Safari Guide

SOUTH AFRICA

Mariëlle Renssen

CONTENTS

GLOBETROTTER™

Safari Guide

SOUTH AFRICA

NEW
HOLLAND

INTRODUCTION

Although South Africa is seen, in the company of its immediate neighbours Namibia and Botswana, as a land of considerable natural beauty and wildlife, it is worth looking at the statistics. A 1996 report issued by the Department of Environmental Affairs and Tourism (a little outdated but some things don't move so fast in this land) confirmed that South Africa's 422 formally protected areas at the time made up a mere 6% of the country. However, that 6% contained 93% of all mammal species and 97% of all bird species in South Africa. Rich land, indeed! The frightening fact is that only 0.6% of the country is covered in indigenous forest, and only 18% of that figure is under conservation – highlighting the dire need for further protectionary measures. The good news is that the Department of Environmental Affairs, with the help of various parks and nature conservation boards such as SANParks and KZN Wildlife, is planning to increase South Africa's protected areas to 10% of its land.

The newly adopted approach of involving and negotiating with cultural communities living on or adjacent to protected land is also to be commended, benefits being that communities are trained and educated in conservation issues, the state is tapping into the community's local knowledge and expertise, and the community shares in the financial rewards of tourism and visitor infrastructure. It all seems a positive way to move into a conservation-focused future.

Top Spots to see Animals

Kruger NP
Pilanesberg NP
Addo Elephant NP
Hluhluwe-iMfolozi NP
Phinda Resource Reserve
Shamwari GR
Mountain Zebra NP

Opposite, top to bottom:
Clear African skies enable visitors to experience the thrill of game-viewing in open-sided vehicles; wetland areas yield the most prolific bird life; tented camps offer accommodation with atmosphere.

Introduction

PART ONE: PLANNING YOUR TRIP

Types of safari
Self-drive

The Kgalagadi Transfrontier National Park and Kruger National Park are two examples of superb nature zones that lend themselves to the self-drive option in your own or a hired rental car. There is a sense of independence, allowing you to plan your days at whim, do your own exploring and work out your own routes. A generally good road network, particularly the tarred routes in Kruger, make most of the parks easily accessible in two-wheel-drive vehicles. Do note that some of the wilder, more remote destinations will need a 4x4 – the tortuously high and serpentine Sani Pass in the Drakensberg, for example. An extensive range of accommodation in most parks gives you the flexibility of multiday stays, and many (although not all) have restaurants, cafeterias or a shop selling basic provisions so you can cook your own meals. Generally, where accommodation includes kitchenettes, these are either partially or fully equipped (see Accommodation at the end of each chapter).

Guided dawn/dusk drives in open 4x4 vehicles

The hot African sun drives most wild animals to seek the shady protection of scrub and trees in the main part of the day. They emerge in the cool hours – early morning and at sunset – to congregate around water holes and along river banks, which makes these the best times to embark on a game drive. Guided excursions are organized by most of the parks, led by highly trained, well-informed rangers and trackers in open-sided vehicles that maximize wildlife-spotting. The tracker sits at the front of the vehicle, his eyes finely attuned to the slightest movement in the surrounding bushveld – the flick of an ear, the switch of a tail – enabling him to alert visitors to a grazing animal. At the more up-market lodges, dawn drives are generally preceded by coffee/tea and rusks/biscuits, followed by a sumptuous breakfast, while dusk excursions usually involve pausing at a scenic spot to toast the sunset, drink in hand.

Night drives in open 4x4 vehicles

Similar to the above excursions, these are undertaken under the cloak of darkness. The tracker carries a spotlight, which he scans in a wide arc across the dark bushveld to catch the

Part One: Planning your trip

Left: Most wildlife reserves conduct both morning and night game drives. Animal viewing is quite different for each — nocturnal animals are only spotted under cover of darkness.

flash of eyes belonging to any of a great number of nocturnal creatures. These animals are active mainly at night, doing their sleeping during the heat of the day and emerging in the darkness to forage and hunt. Many are rarely seen in daylight, which is what makes night drives special. Nocturnal wildlife includes the big cats, particularly leopard and cheetah, as well as smaller feline creatures such as civets, servals and lynxes. Pangolin, aardvark and aardwolf, as well as black-backed jackal and brown and spotted hyena are all nocturnal, so your experience could be an interesting one.

Horseback and elephant-back

Wildlife-viewing on horseback is particularly rewarding as wild animals respond differently to horses, feeling entirely unthreatened by them. This allows you to get a lot closer to ungulates (hoofed animals such as antelope, zebra and giraffe) and even buffalo, rhino and elephant. You can make a faster getaway, too, if it's ever needed! Multiday trails involve overnighting at bush camps,

Top Geological Sites

Table Mountain
Sani Pass
uKhahlamba-Drakensberg
Golden Gate Highlands NP
Karoo NP

Introduction

Suggested Tour Operators

Conservation Corporation (CC)
www.ccafrica.com
tel: +27-(0)11-8094300
e-mail: ceo@ccafrica.com

Wild Frontiers
www.wildfrontiers.com
tel: +27-(0)11-7022035
e-mail: wildfront@icon.co.za

Siyabona Africa
www.nature-reserve.co.za
tel: (+27)-(0)21-4241037
e-mail: reservations@siyabona.com

Southern Africa Places
www.places.co.za
tel: +27-(0)21-8723210/3

and only proficient riders will be permitted to sign up. Most trails are fully catered for, with grooms caring for the horses, although an interest in your mount is appreciated.

Private game reserves go out of their way to give visitors an incomparable safari experience, and Kapama Game Reserve, on Kruger's western border, is one of the few South African reserves to offer dawn or dusk excursions on elephant-back accompanied by experienced rangers and elephant handlers. These usually last no more than a few hours.

Wilderness walking safaris

Walking excursions can vary from morning or evening walks lasting a few hours to full-day walks on wilderness trails spanning two or three days. The longer trails have participants sleeping in tented or rudimentary bush camps deep in the heart of the park's wilderness territory; here you will eat outdoors around a crackling camp fire, stars cartwheeling overhead, the coughs and grunts of wild animals on their night-time prowl clearly audible all about. This is the essence of the bushveld, and it's a thrilling experience. Walking parties are accompanied by armed trackers and guides who are competent, trained and knowledgeable. What's special is taking the time to observe the finer, more subtle details of the bush – listening to bird calls, pausing to watch their behaviour, recognizing spoor and other signs of animals that have recently crossed your path, learning about plants, trees and the geology of the area. This is communicated to you by individuals who have grown up in the bushveld, are tuned in to its subtleties and rhythms and can interpret the most tenuous of signs. It is fascinating and humbling.

4x4 adventure trails

These trails have been established in many of the more rugged parks and nature reserves, and consist of challenging routes over steep, mountainous, rocky terrain or technically difficult sections in remote undeveloped wilderness. Participants use their own vehicles and equipment and need to be entirely self-sufficient; vehicle hire is possible through the major car companies. On the multiday trails, it is advisable that more than one 4x4 travel together in the event of an emergency or a vehicle breakdown.

Part One: Planning your trip

Safari operators

To safeguard your choice of a reputable safari operator, ask whether it has any affiliation to an international organization, such as the International Air Transport Association (IATA), the UK's Air Travel Organisers' Licensing (ATOL), American Society of Travel Agents (ASTA), United States Tour Operators Association (USTOA), or at the very least, the South African Tour Operators Association (SATOA / ASATA).

Note that many safari operators and private game reserves set an age limit for children permitted into the reserve (for your own safety). This is usually under eight, but can extend to age 12.

Conservation fees

All national parks in South Africa charge a conservation fee for every day spent in the park; these fees are payable at the entrance gate office. Conservation fees do not apply to Pilanesberg and parks in KwaZulu-Natal except for the Hluhluwe-iMmfolozi Game Reserve, where the fees form part of accommodation costs. Conservation fees range from R15–R30 for South African residents and R35–R120 for foreigners, depending on the park. Visitors staying for longer than five or six days can join a loyalty programme called Wild Card, which allows them access at a reduced rate. The card can be bought at any of the parks and is valid for one year from date of purchase.

What to pack – clothing

Light, neutral-coloured clothing traditionally served as camouflage in the bushveld in earlier years. To wild animals, neutrals also meld into the surrounding environment, making you less conspicuous and therefore less threatening. Lighter colours also deflect the sun's rays, in contrast to dark hues that absorb heat. The word is, too, that mosquitoes are drawn to darker shades as these act as a good camouflage for the insects. Your suitcase should contain shorts, long trousers and lightweight long-sleeved shirts (for cool nights and as protection against bugs and mosquitoes at night), short-sleeved T-shirts or cool cotton shirts, and a sweater (despite hot breathless days, skies with no cloud cover can cause temperatures to drop sharply at night leaving a distinct chill in the air). A windbreaker is useful, durable light

Binoculars

This is an indispensable safari item, particularly if you're interested in bird-watching. Also, you don't want to be sharing a pair on a game drive where the action can be instantaneous – and fleeting. You can't afford to lose any time when a diffident leopard melts into the roadside shrubbery or a startled rhino hightails it into the veld. Larger, higher magnification binoculars are good for birds but if they're too heavy and unwieldy, you're not going to see much because of hand shake. Aim for something between 7x30 (seven times magnification on a 30mm lens, which determines image brightness) and 10x60.

Introduction

shoes like sneakers as well as hardy walking shoes or boots depending on your type of safari are essential, as is a sun hat or peaked cap to ward off the harsh sun's rays. Also take:
• Good quality polaroid and UVA/UVB radiation-protected sunglasses; the glare of the African sun is particularly bright.
• Lip balm; the dry bushveld air can cause chapped lips.
• Sunscreen with a sun protection factor (SPF) of at least 30 (a reduced ozone layer and the penetrating African sun make anything under 30 inadequate).

Types of accommodation

South African National Parks (SANParks) offers accommodation of all types and standards with prices dependent on location, and the size and quality of the unit. All accommodation has bedding, cooking utensils and refrigeration unless otherwise stated at the end of each chapter. Tariff prices do not include meals. All prices are VAT inclusive. All accommodation, ablution and kitchen facilities are serviced daily by cleaning staff. Camps run by KwaZulu-Natal Wildlife tend to retain camp cooks on site, who will prepare excellent meals from the food provided by the guests.

An adult is rated as 12 years or above. Children (2–11 years) are permitted entry into reserves run by SANParks, but not private reserves (check when booking); children under 2 years are admitted free of charge. No animals may be brought into a national park.

Note that accommodation tends to be booked well in advance (sometimes a year ahead), particularly during peak season (April, July, December/January).

Kruger National Park
Main rest camps
Main rest camps have retail facilities, a restaurant/self-service cafeteria and petrol in the camp (if not, this is available on the park periphery). Main rest camps also have electricity, a first-aid centre, a laundromat/laundry tubs, public telephones, and barbecue and communal kitchen facilities.

Information centres:
Letaba, Skukuza and Berg-en-Dal.

Part One: Planning your trip

Bushveld camps

These are smaller, more remote, more luxurious rest camps with no shops or restaurants. Generally solar-powered (Biyamiti and Bateleur have electricity), but with a refrigerator, stove, crockery, cutlery and cooking utensils. Open verandas often serve as kitchen/dining room. Most bushveld camps organize day excursions and/or night drives.

Communal freezing facilities:

Biyamiti, Shimuwini, Talamati and Sirheni.

Bush lodges or camps

Kruger has two bush lodges, Boulders and Roodewal, which have to be reserved as a single booking. Exclusive, private and decorated in ethnic style, they have fully equipped kitchens plus gas braais and barbecue facilities. There are no shops or restaurant facilities.

Bungalows

These round, thatched, single-roomed African-style (rondavel) units contain 2–3 beds with a shower or bath en suite; most are air conditioned. Kitchenettes vary, some with hotplates, cutlery and crockery; visitors should check when booking. Luxury bungalows on a river frontage are slightly more up-market, with glass sliding doors.

Left: Situated in mopane veld some 50km (30 miles) from the Punda Maria Rest Camp, Sirheni Camp lines the shore of a dam sharing the same name, and fed by the Mphongolo River. Rustic in nature, electricity is provided via solar panels. A hide on the perimeter fence, overlooking the dam, enables sneak peaks at the bushveld bird life and animals traipsing to the water's edge.

Introduction

Above: Camping facilities exist in most wildlife reserves. A popular and cost-effective form of accommodation, camping also brings you into closer contact with nature.

Rondavels

These round, thatched, one-bedroom units are either self-equipped or share communal facilities.

Huts

Consisting of one room, each hut makes use of communal ablution and kitchen facilities. Only Orpen's huts have basic cooking utensils, crockery and cutlery; other camp huts require visitors to be fully self-sufficient.

Guesthouses

See below.

Cottages/Family and guest cottages

See page 15.

Tents/camping

See page 15.

Other National Park/Safari Destinations
Guesthouses

Secluded units within a rest camp, they have 3 or 4 bedrooms, most en suite, a fully equipped kitchen and share a communal living room or open veranda.

Part One: Planning your trip

Cottages

These stand-alone units comprise a bedroom, living room, bathroom and partially equipped kitchen or kitchenette. Family cottages have one, two or three bedrooms and a fully equipped kitchen.

Guest cottages

These 2- to 3-bedroom units have at least two bathrooms, one en suite, and a fully equipped kitchen.

Chalets

Semi-detached open-plan units, these contain one or more bedrooms; larger units are known as family chalets.

Chalavans

This resembles a permanent caravan-cum-cottage; some are self-equipped, others share communal ablution facilities.

Forest huts/cabins

The huts are budget, single-room furnished units with 2 or 4 beds; they share a communal kitchen and ablution facilities. The cabins are similar, but are fully equipped.

Tents (safari, desert, tent camps)

These permanent canvas tent units, on wooden platforms, are equipped with beds, a cupboard, table and chairs, fridge and electric fan. Some of them come with a fully equipped kitchenette (for example Kgalagadi Transfrontier National Park), others have communal kitchen and ablution facilities (Kruger National Park). Tents at Punda Maria contain a bathroom with shower, a kitchenette (with fridge) on the verandah and a braai stand. One unit has been adapted for physically impaired visitors.

Camping/caravanning

Most parks offer this facility. Each site allows a maximum of 6 persons, I vehicle and I caravan with side tent; or a maximum of I vehicle and 2 tents; or I autovilla; or I motorized caravan. Sites are equipped with power points, but in some cases this applies to a portion of the site only; check when booking. Visitors may use generators only in daylight (I hour after sunrise to I hour before sunset). All camps offer communal kitchen and ablution facilities.

Introduction

Websites to Research your Safari

* South African National Parks (SANParks), www.sanparks.org (go to: Parks A–Z)
* KwaZulu-Natal Wildlife (KZN Wildlife), www.kznwildlife.com
* Siyabona Africa, www.nature-reserve.co.za
* Southern Africa Places, www.places.co.za
* Bird life: SANParks site on bird species for each national park, www.sanparks.org/groups/birders or www.birdlife.org.za www.sabirding.co.za

Park etiquette
Respect what's wild

• Loud voices and aggressive behaviour are only going to send wildlife scampering off into the wilderness. On any driving or walking excursion, keep voices low and conversation to a minimum. Stay in your vehicle or close by your guide unless advised otherwise.

• Never try to interfere with animal behaviour by shouting, clapping, imitating their sound or throwing stones, and never ever get in the way of an animal's escape route or between an animal and its young. This is particularly true of an elephant cow and her babies or a hippo trying to get to water. Both are highly protective of their young and their territory and will turn ferocious if threatened in any way.

• Respect the commands of your guides and trackers as their experience makes them far more knowledgeable than you in the event of a crisis. Above all, don't ask them to let you get closer to a wild animal than the distance they feel comfortable with; animal behaviour can be wholly unpredictable and this can endanger your lives, particularly if an individual feels threatened. Getting too close can also obstruct a hunt and force the animal to abandon its chase, denying it a meal.

• If you're out game-viewing in your own car, approach animals carefully, quietly and calmly. Sudden movements or a panic-stricken retreat will get more of an aggressive reaction out of an animal – particularly elephant and rhino – than a slow, calm reversal out of charging distance.

• Never approach a wild animal on foot unless you are being guided by an expert on a walking trail.

• Don't feed animals such as baboons, monkeys or those that have become habituated around camps, such as jackals, mongooses, and so on. This interferes with their natural habits and can make them dependent on camp food.

• Respect the environment; don't throw litter into the wild. Certain items can choke or poison animals and birds. Never smoke on a game drive and never, ever toss a burning cigarette into the bush; the dry vegetation ignites easily and this could cause a highly destructive veld fire. This is a very real problem in South Africa, and has resulted in major devastation of both environment and animal life.

PART TWO: ECO ISSUES AND CLIMATE

Topography

Physically, South Africa is defined by three major topographical features – a huge central plateau that takes up most of the country, a low-lying coastal band fringing the entire subcontinent and, separating the two, a rugged range of massively buckled and folded mountains. Beginning with the Eastern Escarpment west of Kruger, this range curves through the Drakensberg chain, then sweeps all the way to a series of parallel-lying Cape Fold Mountains bounding the southwestern coastline.

Climate

Climatically, South Africa's summer begins around mid-October lasting till mid-February, after which a less-defined autumn of usually balmy, warm and sunny days leads into the winter months, lasting from May to end July. Summers generally are sun-filled and hot throughout the country, with very high humidity in KwaZulu-Natal and the northern parts of the country, particularly around Kruger and the Blyde River Canyon. The country experiences summer rainfall (the Western Cape is the only exception), and on the central highveld plateau, regular thunderstorms reverberate dramatically overhead as lightning slashes the sky open. In contrast, winters on the highveld are dry, with crisp cool mornings and evenings, very chilly nights but gloriously mild clear days. Spring, from August to mid-October, is heralded in, from the country's top to its tip, by multitudes of wild flowers turning their pretty bright faces to the sun. They are at their most splendid in the Western Cape, but the landscapes of the country's arid interior and the Drakensberg are also sprinkled with a kaleidoscope of vivid blooms. The high mountain peaks of the Cape and Drakensberg are often iced with snow during the winter months, causing air temperatures to plummet by several degrees. There is a weather reversal in the Western Cape – the only region to experience a Mediterranean climate. This means heavy winter rainfall, often brought by storms together with lashing wind and icy rain. The Cape's spring and early summer months are characterized by the notorious Southeaster, a wild, often gale-force wind that rips around the coastline sometimes for days on end.

**Top Spots for
Spring Flowers**

Table Mountain NP/Kirstenbosch
Golden Gate NP
Karoo NP

Introduction

Best times to visit South Africa

The Cape is at its best in spring (August–mid-October) and in the balmy autumn months of February–March; beach-goers will love the hot, blue-sky (but very busy) months of December–January. KwaZulu-Natal's warm, dry, subtropical winters (June–August) when summer's humidity is absent make this a perfect time to visit. The warmer waters of the Indian Ocean make swimming pleasant, even in winter. The country's northern regions (including the Northern, Mpumalanga, and Limpopo provinces) are best in winter – May through July – because they can be exceptionally hot in summer, and winter days are clear, sunny and pleasantly warm. In terms of game-viewing, the dry winters witness the deciduous bushveld trees losing their leaves, improving viewing visibility considerably, and there are also fewer watering points for wildlife to congregate at, so targeting the main water holes usually produces great results. Summers, with their high rainfall, encourage a profusion of luxuriant growth, resulting in dense tangled vegetation that makes it extremely difficult to see the animals. Camouflage is at its most effective and only the most trained eye can separate a dappled coat or hide from the leafy backdrop. Rivers and streams are also replenished and full, so water is bountiful throughout the parks making it difficult to pinpoint specific watering points that are likely to yield game sightings.

Below: *Sensitively constructed bird hides enable keen birders to spy unobtrusively on the activities of the bushveld's multitude of feathered creatures.*

Part Two: Eco issues and climate

Bird-watching

Of interest to twitchers are the months of October to December (spring/summer), the most satisfying for birding, although Southern Africa's less defined seasons make bird-watching possible all year round. In the spring months of September–October, Bald Ibis chicks arrive and Denham's (Stanley's) Bustard males put on their enormous white-chested displays. Palaearctic migrants, arriving from Siberia and northern China, India and North Africa, visit Southern African shores from December to March to evade bitter northern hemisphere winters. Summer is also good for high-wheeling raptors, particularly Walhberg's Eagle, Steppe Eagle and Lesser Spotted Eagle.

Top Spots to see Birds

Pilanesberg
Punda Maria, northern Kruger
Lower Sabie, southeastern Kruger
Mapungubwe
Kgalagadi
Greater St Lucia Wetlands
Mkhuze GR (KZN)
Ndumo GR (KZN)
Hluhluwe-iMfolozi

Whale-watching

Southern right and humpback whales breed and calve in Southern African waters from mid-June to the end of October.

Turtle breeding season

October to March is nesting season in KwaZulu-Natal for leatherback and loggerhead turtles, and visitor tours are conducted during December–January.

Environmental organizations

Many of South Africa's protected areas have received international recognition as conservation-worthy regions. Below are brief profiles of the most important of these organizations.

UNESCO (United Nations Educational, Scientific, and Cultural Organization) designates Biosphere Reserves and World Heritage Sites. A biosphere reserve is where conservation and both human land use and activity complement one another; it is also sustainable in the long term. A protected core area is left purely for conservation, while a carefully managed surrounding buffer zone allows human activity with a strong emphasis on community involvement. The local community is educated and trained on conservation issues, but it also benefits from the profits gained through tourism. With this comes social upliftment and rural development. Website: whc.unesco.org/en/about

IUCN (World Conservation Union) is responsible for identifying the risks of global extinction in plants, animals, birds – all living organisms.

Introduction

The IUCN Red List catalogues and highlights those species at risk of extinction in terms of: Threatened, Vulnerable, Endangered and Critically Endangered. Website: www.iucnredlist.org

Ramsar is a convention that was signed in Ramsar, Iran, in 1971 to preserve the world's wetlands. The Convention on Wetlands provides a framework for the conservation and wise use of wetlands and their resources, and for ensuring that sustainable development is achieved. Significant wetland areas of the world are registered on the Ramsar List of Wetlands of International Importance. Website: www.ramsar.org

Habitats and biomes

Both topography and climate determine the country's main vegetation zones. These zones, made up of a predominant vegetation type, contain life forms that have adapted to that particular environment and its vegetation, and are known as biomes. In turn, an ecosystem is a community of adapted organisms, so several ecosystems exist within a biome. Although ecologists do not always agree on the precise number of biomes in South Africa (they are often defined by climate characteristics or alternatively by life-form species), there are at least seven major biomes. These are *Fynbos*, Savannah, Grassland, Nama-Karoo, Succulent Karoo, Forest and Marine/Wetlands (not indicated on the map, page 21).

Fynbos

This evergreen, narrow-leaved heathland and shrubland covers 5.3 % of South Africa, but is strictly limited to the Western Cape.

Below, left and right: South Africa's diversity is evident in these two contrasting landscapes – a flat, dry expanse of the Karoo softened by a show of pretty drought-resistant spring flowers (left) and the verdant, leafy depths of Knysna's indigenous forest – among the last original tracts in the country.

Part Two: Eco issues and climate

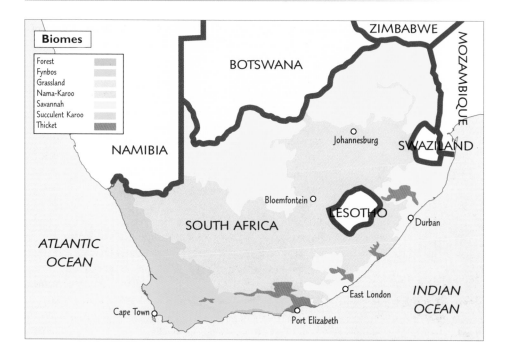

Biomes

Forest	
Fynbos	
Grassland	
Nama-Karoo	
Savannah	
Succulent Karoo	
Thicket	

ZIMBABWE

MOZAMBIQUE

BOTSWANA

NAMIBIA

Johannesburg

SWAZILAND

Bloemfontein

LESOTHO

SOUTH AFRICA

Durban

ATLANTIC OCEAN

East London

INDIAN OCEAN

Cape Town

Port Elizabeth

It includes proteas, ericas and restios – a group of leafless tufted grasses. In winter and spring/summer, *fynbos* produces an enormous range of woody, tufted flowers and coloured leaves that range from sunshine yellows through rosy pinks to sunset oranges and reds. *Fynbos* comprises at least 8578 species of flowering plants, 68% endemic (that is, occurring nowhere else in the world) to the Cape. These plants pollinate via birds and small animals. They are regularly visited by long-tailed Cape Sugarbirds and Orange-breasted Sunbirds.

Succulent Karoo

This biome experiences intensely arid summers with sparse rainfall in winter. It occurs along the western belt of the Western Cape and inland towards the Little Karoo and produces the West Coast's myriad spring flowers. Succulent plants with thick, fleshy leaves, such as the Stone Plant (*Lithops* spp.), geophytes (bulbs, corms and tubers), Kokerboom or Quiver Tree (*Aloe dichotoma*) and Halfmens (*Pachypodium namaquanum*) survive in this arid

Introduction

region. It's also the territory of the bat-eared fox and the common barking gecko.

Nama-Karoo

This biome forms a transition zone between the Cape flora and tropical savannah; it occurs across the vast central plateau area occupied by the Western and Northern Cape. There is a crossover of plant species from other zones, but aloes, euphorbias, sweet-thorn acacias and blue Karoo Daisies (*Felicia australis*) are prevalent. Vast flocks of sheep and goats have replaced the one-time springbok herds.

Savannah

Savannah vegetation includes wooded grasslands featuring Mopane (*Colophospermum mopane*) and a huge range of acacia species such as Monkey-thorn (*Acacia galpini*) and Knob-thorn (*A. nigrescens*) as well as valley bushveld. It makes up 46% of the South African landscape and supports the country's sought-after larger wildlife species such as elephant, buffalo and lion.

Grassland

These areas, where grasses are dominant and there is a distinct lack of woody plants, occupy 24% of South Africa's land area. They exist on the high central plateau, KwaZulu-Natal's midland areas and the mountain zones of the Eastern Cape. Climatic conditions contributing to this vegetation zone are summer thunderstorms, often accompanied by hail, and frosty winters. *Themeda triandra*, or Red Grass, is widespread, attracting ungulates (hoofed animals) such as wildebeest, zebra, kudu and springbok.

Forest

Indigenous evergreen and semi-deciduous forests, scattered in the higher rainfall zones, cover only 0.25% of South African territory. The most extensive are the indigenous tracts of Knysna and the Wilderness and Tsitsikamma forests (yellowwood, stinkwood and ironwood) and KwaZulu-Natal's coastal dune forests of Alexandria. The total area adds up to less than 2000km² (772 sq miles). Tiny blue duiker and bushbuck, as well as bushpig, live beneath the forest canopy, and brilliant-plumed birds such as Knysna Turaco (Lourie) and Narina Trogon flit between the branches.

Part Two: Eco issues and climate

Marine coastline and Wetlands

South Africa's coastline extends for over 3000km (1864 miles), consisting mainly of sandy beaches and sand dunes, but including the ecosystems of rocky shores, coral reefs, kelp beds and the open sea. The intertidal zone supports creatures such as the plough snail, white mussel and pink ghost crab, while leatherback and loggerhead turtles breed here. The country's only coral reefs exist in the subtropical environment of northern KwaZulu-Natal and Maputaland. These offshore waters are also rich in large deep-sea fish species. The cold waters of the Cape's western coastline, on the other hand, feature dense beds of giant kelp or sea bamboo, supporting rock lobster and abalone (perlemoen).

Wetlands span both inland and coastal habitats that encompass marshes, swamps and estuaries, all linked to rivers and streams. Subtropical coastal vegetation features mangroves, palms and strelitzias such as Natal wild banana. In marshy areas, reeds and bulrushes form an ecosystem that creates organic matter and oxygenates soil and water, at the same time sustaining enormous numbers of water birds. Among these species are Pink-backed Pelican, Rufous-bellied Heron, Open-billed Stork and Pygmy Goose.

Above: The African Jacana has particularly long toes and nails, designed for walking over floating vegetation such as these water lily pads.

PILANESBERG NATIONAL PARK

Limpopo

Pilanesberg
National Park

Rustenburg•

North West

Johannesburg•

Gauteng

Measured against all other South African national parks, Pilanesberg is singularly unique in its location, elevated as it is on the remnants of an extinct volcanic crater. Four broken concentric rings of rocky hills, buffeted, scoured and eroded by the elements over aeons, create a natural border for the reserve cradled within. Their near-perfect circular imprint on the landscape – forming a diameter of some 25km (15 miles) – makes this ancient volcanic site globally significant. It has been labelled the Pilanesberg Alkaline Ring Complex, indicating that the volcano, which erupted roughly 1300 million years ago, was alkaline in composition and structure (see panel, page 30). It is also the third largest alkaline ring complex in the world. Scientists estimate that, through both extrusion and intrusion (during which searing magma first penetrates cracks in the earth's crust, then forces its way into solid rock), the volcanic cone eventually formed by the solidified lava rose to 7000m (23,000ft). With the passing of the ages, further eruptions, fracturing and elemental weathering caused the collapse of the cone, producing the gigantic caldera. It's possible that Mankwe Lake, centred within the ancient crater, was the source of the main volcanic pipe. Today the highest upland is Pilanesberg Peak, touching on 600m (1970ft).

Park Statistics

Location: 50km (30 miles) from Rustenburg; ±180km (110 miles) from Johannesburg.

Size: 550km² (212 sq miles).

5-star factor: Thanks to Operation Genesis, all indigenous large mammals of the area are represented here.

Of interest: Unique geological structure of the ancient alkaline ring-dyke volcanic crater on which the park is established.

*Opposite, top and bottom:
Elephant (top) and both black
and white rhino (bottom) are
among the Big Five species
introduced into Pilanesberg.
Opposite, centre: Mankwe
Lake is the centre of a collapsed
volcanic cone.*

Pilanesberg National Park

Animal Life

All of the Big Five: *see panel, page 8* (both Black and White rhino)

The meat-eaters
Cheetah
Wild dog
Brown hyena
Black-backed jackal

The vegetarians
Giraffe
Blue wildebeest
Red hartebeest
Tsessebe
Waterbuck
Kudu

The mean-horned
Gemsbok
Sable antelope

They came in two by two ...

Pilanesberg's mountain range takes its name from Chief Pilane of the Bakgatla clan belonging to the Tswana people, one-time rulers of the area. Before 1979, Pilanesberg's territory had been reduced to denuded, overgrazed farmland. In that year, it was proclaimed a national park and the authorities immediately set about redressing the effects of erosion, removing alien plants and establishing indigenous trees and shrubs, and even diverting telephone wires.

Yet more ambitious was the implementation of Operation Genesis, a plan to translocate over 6000 head of wildlife – a total of 19 different species – into the new reserve. White and black rhino were reintroduced from KwaZulu-Natal, elephant and buffalo from Addo Elephant Park, and Burchell's zebra and waterbuck arrived from Mpumalanga. Giraffe and eland were transported from as far afield as Namibia. This major effort has translated into a park today that demands to be taken seriously. Its wealth of wildlife presents all the indigenous animals that once historically existed here.

Right: Clearly delineating the giraffe's horizon are Pilanesberg's volcanic hills, remnants of an ancient crater.

Domain of diversity

A road network of close to 200km (125 miles) allows visitors to thread their way across the hilly crater, encountering grassland, bushveld and woodland animal species. Unfortunately, the well-known Mothata Scavenger Hide that used to exist near Manyane Gate in the east is no longer operational as a result of the presence of lion in the park! The competition has proved a little too hot to handle for the vultures. Nevertheless, species you could still spot circling overhead are Cape Vultures, which nest in the Magaliesberg's rugged cliffs, and White-backed and Lappet-faced Vultures. The Cape and White-backed species feature the characteristic featherless 'bald'-looking head and neck with a ruff of collar-feathers at the base; impressive hooked beaks hint at their favoured diet. The Lappet-faced vulture is one species you'll have no problem in identifying. The paintbrush was generous here in its selection of colour palette – a black feather ruff encircles the base of a purple- and crimson-tinted head and neck. Marabou Storks might just also put in an appearance – these giant long-legged birds share the vultures' absence of head and neck feathers, and carry a pink fleshy pouch on the front lower neck below a great jabbing beak, hugely to be reckoned with.

Domain of diversity

The Pilanesberg National Park straddles a vegetational transition zone between dry Kalahari habitats and the moister, higher rainfall habitat of the Lowveld zone. Vegetation types therefore fall into the Grassland and Savannah biomes – bushveld country with occasional thickly forested ravines and wooded pockets of land. What makes it interesting is the juxtaposition of, for example, wiry Camel-thorns (*Acacia erioloba*) with leafy large-canopied Cape Chestnut (*Calodendrum capense*) trees.

Typical trees making an appearance include Umbrella (*A. tortilis*) and Common Hook-thorn (*A. caffra*) acacias, leathery, narrow-leaved Wild Olives (*Olea europaea*) and the pretty – in spring, that is – Common Wild Pear (*Dombeya rotundifolia*) whose bare branches are smothered in white or pink blossoms. Worth looking out for is the intriguingly named Transvaal Red Balloon Tree (*Erythrophysa transvaalensis*). Reasonably rare, there are only a few belts occurring in the North West province, eking out an existence on rock koppies or stony hillsides. The tree gets its playful name from inflated, three-sided capsules graded green to red that hang off the end of the branches from

Bird Life

360+ SPECIES
Legal eagles
Tawny Eagle
Martial Eagle
African Hawk Eagle
Wahlberg's Eagle
Verreaux's Eagle
Black-breasted Snake Eagle
Wise owls
Grass Owl
Pearl-spotted Owl
Spotted Eagle Owl
Leggy birds
Kori Bustard
White-winged Korhaan
Red-crested Korhaan
All decked out
Lilac-breasted Roller
Crimson-breasted Shrike
Black-collared Barbet
Violet-eared Waxbill

Pilanesberg National Park

October to February. These fruits are preceded by brick-red flower sprays.

Pilanesberg's great expansive grassland plains and knobbly knuckled green-mantled hills can be experienced in any of several ways: hikers are taken deep into the park by trained knowledgeable guides for three-hour walks; or dawn, dusk and night game drives are conducted in high open vehicles, followed by a hearty breakfast or dinner lit by myriad stars and a roaring wood fire, with the calls of wild animals your only background entertainment. Otherwise, if independence is your game, the road network is extensive and the Geological Auto Trail inducts you into the rock structure's secrets of lava, cones and craters – if you buy the related booklet sold at the Manyane tourist complex, that is.

The cherry on the top (if your pockets are deep enough) is to get a thermal-riding perspective on Pilanesberg's landscape from a giant hot-air balloon. Launching in the gilded glow of dawn's light, you drift silently, soundlessly, over the plains, too unobtrusive to startle the waking wildlife. The only sound in your ears is the intermittent roar of the gas burners as they

Africa's Painted Dogs

The African wild dog is at present an endangered species for various reasons. Its roaming habits have brought it up against farmers and their livestock while, until the 1960s, even game rangers targeted wild dogs for their propensity to disturb small antelope herds (which, at the time, were considered more important in terms of conservation). Wild dog behaviour has been compared to that of northern hemisphere wolves, and it plays a similar role in weeding out weak and unhealthy animals from the antelope population. Wild dogs in fact kill and eat their prey – impala, grey duiker, steenbok – much more efficiently than other predators. Their large rounded ears afford them a highly acute sense of hearing. When greeting one another or when excited, they make a high-pitched twittering sound; otherwise, if the pack is split up, they communicate with a hooting (or 'whoo') call.

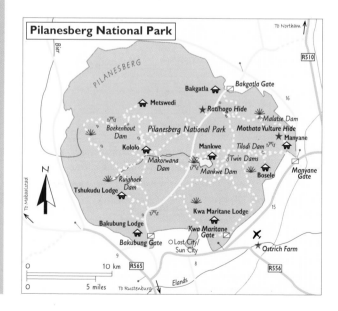

Accommodation

keep the balloon filled with heated air. After being suspended above earth for anything up to an hour, the exhilaration of a gently bumpy touchdown is enhanced by the bubbles of a glass of sparkling wine; next is a sumptuous breakfast at one of the lodges. An irresistible mix.

Above: Pilanesberg by hot-air balloon – a unique (and non-invasive) approach to gazing at the bemused wildlife foraging below.

When to visit

Summers are hot (average 35°C/95°F); rain falls Oct–Mar. Winters (May–Sep) are better as wildlife concentrates at water holes; night temperatures can fall to below zero. Gate opening times: Apr–Aug 06:00–18:00; Sep–Mar 05:30–19:00.

Accommodation

Manyane Resort

Luxury chalets: thatched, Africa-inspired décor, some with loft bedroom; fully catered; two pools; mini-golf.

Pilanesberg National Park

Delving into Volcanic Alkalinity

As far as scientists can make out, alkaline volcanoes are known to give off enormous quantities of carbon dioxide. The experts believe that before humans fouled the atmosphere with industrial pollution, volcanoes were responsible for emitting carbon dioxide into the air – all part of a natural process that involves sea water absorbing it as well as carbon dioxide's contribution to the photosynthesis cycle of all plants. Unusual rock types, often containing high concentrations of particular elements and also rare earth elements, have been detected too in alkaline volcanoes. In the case of Pilanesberg, the volcanic rock is particularly high in sodium and potassium, and lacking in silica.

Self-catering chalets: brick and thatch, air conditioning; private patio and braai facilities, resort pool.

Safari tents: for two persons, overlooking the bushveld, electrified, with communal ablutions. Self-catering or breakfast/dinner options.

Camp sites: caravan and camping facilities.

Bakgatla Resort

Chalets: at foot of Bakgatla hills; brick with zinc roof, colonial-style décor, additional loft bedroom; air conditioning, private patio and braai facilities; resort salt-water pool.

Camp sites: caravan and camping facilities.

Tshukudu Lodge (Place of the rhino)

Six wooden-beamed, thatched A-frame luxury units peep out of tall trees from high on a hill (there are 132 steps to climb up to the lodge!). Private balcony, overlooks water hole, stupendous views. Best feature is sizable oval bath beside windows thrown open to rolling plains spread below and green hills marching to where earth meets sky. Rock plunge pool, resort activities.

Bakubung Lodge (Place of the hippo)

This thatched complex tightly hugs a wooded hill and looks onto a reed-fringed pool where, as the name suggests, hippo once hid out. A parade of wildlife does venture to its banks, though, clearly visible from the lodge. Tall, narrow, thatched studio rooms huddle closely together against the hill like a row of Carmine Bee-eaters hugging a cliff; there is also a horseshoe curve of self-catering chalets. An aquamarine pool has giant boulders piled high at its centre; there is also a restaurant, a *lapa* under the stars, and a variety of resort activities.

Kwa Maritane Lodge (Place of the rock)

The name alludes to the solidified magma foundations this lodge is built upon. This complex is built of natural materials – stone, wooden beams and thatch; A-frame luxury rooms tucked into the trees, with wooded hills of igneous rock rearing up all around. Restaurant, 2 sparkling blue pools, resort facilities.

Opposite: Bakubung Lodge's horseshoe of chalets curves around a rock-dominated pool.

Contact details

Contact details

Manyane and Bakgatla
Golden Leopard Resorts
tel: +27-(0)14-5551000, e-mail: goldres@iafrica.com
website: www.goldenleopard.co.za

Kwa Maritane
Legacy Hotels and Resorts
tel: +27-(0)14-5525100/5200
e-mail: kwamaritane@legacyhotels.co.za
website: www.legacyhotels.co.za/Home.aspx

Bakubung
tel: +27-(0)14-5526000
e-mail: bakubung@legacyhotels.co.za

Tshukudu
tel: +27-(0)14-5526255
e-mail: tshukudu@legacyhotels.co.za

For great images of accommodation and also reservations:
www.places.co.za/html/4680.html

Sun City

Right next door to Pilanesberg National Park, of course, is the jangly, bright-lights world of casinos and near-naked, feather-boa-clad dancers at Sun City. The Palace of the Lost City will have you marvelling open-mouthed at its opulence and fantastical architecture, with cupolas, domes and wildlife sculptures. It seems the artificially generated rollers at the Roaring Lagoon are good enough to surf ...

KRUGER NATIONAL PARK AND BLYDE RIVER CANYON NATURE RESERVE

The Kruger National Park is South Africa's biggest wildlife reserve and falls into the 10 largest sanctuaries of the world. Although its earliest beginnings were fraught with intense resistance and heated power struggles, its success today has reached such proportions that the danger of overpopulation exists among some mammal species.

The threat of overpopulation concerns elephants, in particular. From an estimated number of 25 in 1912, today's figure is not much short of 11,700 giant grey pachyderms. Various sensitive measures are presently underway to control the numbers.

The park today extends for 345km (215 miles) north to south, and on average measures roughly 55km (35 miles) across. There is an astounding 3000km (1863 miles) of road for self-drive touring fanatics to explore, given time and patience.

Park Statistics

Location: Main gateway to park, Malelane Gate (Southern Kruger) is ±75km (47 miles) from Nelspruit.
Size: 20,000km², or 19,685km² to be exact (7600 sq miles).
5-star factor: Big Five in mammals, Big Five in birds, Big Five in trees.
Of interest: Formation of Greater Limpopo Transfrontier Park in 2002 makes the 35,000km² (13,500-sq-mile) reserve one of the largest in the world.

Opposite top: Only the male lion carries a majestic mane.
Opposite centre: Letaba Camp is set in mopane veld in central Kruger.
Opposite bottom: Frisky, sinuous-necked giraffe.

Kruger National Park

Kruger, Stevenson-Hamilton and Grobler

The reserve's origins go back to the unlikely figure of Paul Kruger, a sixth-generation staunch Afrikaner who became the president of the South African Republic in 1883. In spite of his cultural heritage and, indeed, his own initial stubborn resistance, it dawned painfully on him that his Voortrekker forebears had been responsible for the decimation of enormous populations of game during hunting forays in the Transvaal from the 1830s onward. Needless to say, it took from 1884, when the idea was broached, to 1898 to found the Sabi Game Reserve, cradled by the Crocodile and Sabie rivers.

Enter the man most credited with laying the foundations of the park as it is now, Lieutenant-Colonel James Stevenson-Hamilton. He was appointed head ranger by Paul Kruger in 1902 and outstripped his contemporaries with a vision that was way ahead of its time. Making himself a slew of enemies, Stevenson-Hamilton ruthlessly took on illegal squatters, poachers and cavalier hunters, earning himself the nickname *Sikhukhuza* by the local Tsonga. Translated variously as 'he who levels the ground' (some say

Right: Female kudus do not carry horns; only the male sports the dramatic spiralled horns seen here.

Greater Limpopo Transfrontier Park

'sweeps clean') or 'he who turns everything upside down', the name has evolved over time into 'Skukuza' which today is the name of Kruger's main camp and headquarters.

In the 44 years that Stevenson-Hamilton headed up the reserve, he battled constantly to change the entrenched attitudes of hunters, miners and agriculturalists who believed that the land should be subdivided into farms, grazing areas and land for industry. He succeeded in extending the reserve to the Olifants River (roughly the halfway mark of today's Kruger National Park). In the same year, 1903, the government agreed to protect a huge tract of land lining the Lebombo mountains – from the Letaba River, which joins the Olifants River, to the Luvuvhu River in the extreme north. This was given the name Shingwedzi Game Reserve.

It was only when public awareness grew, perceptions improved and the opinions of even certain government members were swayed that Stevenson-Hamilton had any further joy. In 1926, Minister of Lands Piet Grobler eventually introduced the National Parks Act, and the Sabi and Shingwedzi game reserves, together with the land in between, became the Kruger National Park. It was not much different then from today's full extent of the park.

Greater Limpopo Transfrontier Park

In December 2002, the signing of an international treaty between three heads of state involved a ground-breaking move to merge the national reserves of three African countries. And so the seeds were sown for the establishment of the Greater Limpopo Transfrontier Park which, when all the fences have been lowered between the three countries to promote unrestricted movement of people and migration of wildlife across the borders, will be one of the largest sanctuaries in the world.

The treaty proclaimed the linking of Kruger with Mozambique's Limpopo National Park and Zimbabwe's Gonarezhou National Park as well as its Manjinji Pan Sanctuary and Malipati Safari Area, adding up to a total area of around 35,000km² (13,515 sq miles). It will comprise 58% South African, 24% Mozambican and 18% Zimbabwean territory.

Bird Life

Southern Zone
Brown-headed Parrot
White-browed Robin-chat
  (Heuglin's Robin)
Scarlet-chested Sunbird
Purple-crested Turaco (Lourie)
Lilac-breasted Roller

Central Zone
Tawny Eagle
Bateleur
Black-shouldered Kite
Martial Eagle

River Zones
Goliath Heron
Giant Kingfisher
African Fish Eagle
Verreaux's (Giant) Eagle Owl
Pel's Fishing Owl
Trumpeter Hornbill

Kruger National Park

Bridging areas, consisting of the Sengwe communal land in Zimbabwe and Kruger's northernmost wedge between the Luvuvhu and Limpopo rivers – today the Makuleke Concession area – are also part of the transfrontier park. In a historic agreement a few years ago, the Makuleke people were granted the rights to their ancestral lands, defined by these two rivers.

Today, in partnership with park authorities and also Wilderness Safaris, who have built a luxury tented lodge in the Makuleke/Pafuri area, the Makuleke people have undergone extensive training in conservation matters. They also participate in the management of the area, benefiting from tourism and community development projects.

The transfrontier park will take a number of years to become fully operational. In the meantime, the Pafuri border post with Mozambique opened in 2002 together with a symbolic removal of fencing between the Shingwedzi River and the new border post. Then in December 2005, the Giriyondo border post with Mozambique was opened and a 30km (18½-mile) section of fencing was removed, this time south of Shingwedzi.

Kruger has been able to find an alternative solution to its burgeoning elephant population by translocating surplus numbers into Mozambique, at the same time hoping to encourage natural transmigration between the two countries; it appears this is happening successfully. Ten white rhino were also introduced into the Limpopo National Park. It is unfortunate that Zimbabwe's economic crisis is hampering that country's progress in terms of infrastructure and facilities, and the lack of a direct road network at the time of writing was making it difficult for visitors to cross into Gonarezhou. Poaching is also an issue that won't quite go away, creating ongoing headaches for park officials in all three countries.

Diverse landscapes and ecozones aplenty

Rivers play a significant role in Kruger country, defining the north and south boundaries and also dividing the park decisively into four major landscapes – although the diversity of this territory embraces up to 35 identified landscape types. Of Kruger's seven

Diverse landscapes and ecozones aplenty

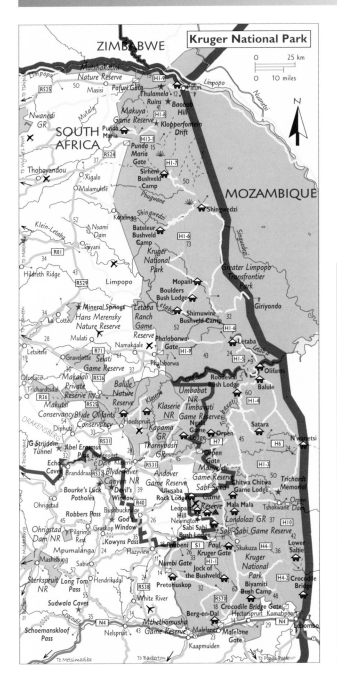

Did you know?

• The larger skull and thick coarse-haired mane of a male lion protect it from blows to the head, both from struggling prey and rival males; head clashing is part of male territorial behaviour.

• A giraffe's neck consists of seven vertebrae, each one 30cm (1ft) long. Two male giraffes willl bump and entwine their sinuous necks as a show of dominance that ends when both animals are too tired to continue.

• The black-and-white stripes of a zebra's coat are not a fashion item; they create a confusing dark and light maze to predators who battle to identify single individuals to target and bring down.

Kruger National Park

Baobab
Marula
Mopane
Fever Tree
Knob-thorn

major rivers, five flow all year round. In the extreme north, the Limpopo separates South Africa and Zimbabwe; in the far south, the park bounds are marked by the Crocodile River. The Olifants River cuts right across the centre of Kruger with the Letaba splaying off at an angle, cutting a perfect triangular wedge in the middle of the park. Rainfall steadily decreases northward to the Limpopo boundary.

Another distinctive feature is a north–south split that sees the west length of the park dominated by granitic rock, while the east length is characterized by volcanic basalt and shales. This basalt contains iron, magnesium, calcium and phosphate, all of which act as a rich nutrient base for the grasslands concentrated here. The basalt also holds water well, explaining why grazers (and their predators) are constantly drawn to this section of the park.

The park's rivers are an ever-present cause for concern to conservationists as agricultural, mining and forestry industries have taken a heavy toll, and their water flow has been substantially reduced over the years. Reassuringly, Kruger has a full-time presence of scientists researching its ecosystem, in collaboration with other scientific experts from around the world.

Below: The Sabie River cradles the southernmost – and more popular – sector of Kruger.

Kruger's three sectors

Extreme southern sector (between Crocodile and Sabie)

Distinctive to this area, particularly around the camps of Pretoriuskop, Berg-en-Dal and Malelane to the west, are rounded granite hills rising out of dense bush savannah, made up mainly of different types of Bushwillow (*Combretum* spp.) and Silver Cluster-leaf (*Terminalia sericea*) woodland. Petite and incredibly sure-footed klipspringer and mountain reedbuck love the rocky bouldered terrain. The cluster-leaf trees are easy to identify by the clutch of silvery silky-haired leaves carried on each stem; the tree often carries dried red-brown winged pods which degenerate into a twisted, tangled mass. Bushwillow species, notably Large-fruited (*Combretum zeyheri*) and Red Bushwillow (*C. apiculatum*), also carry pod-like winged fruit, this time with four papery wings. Pale green when young, they mature to brown.

Other tree species that are conspicuous in this park sector are Horned Thorn (*Acacia grandicornuta*) with its thin, woody, sickle-curved pods, and the ubiquitous butterfly-leaved Mopane (*Colophospermum mopane*).

The African landscape gets its splashes of colour via the Red Bauhinia (*Bauhinia galpinii*) – also known as pride-of-the-Kaap, its loveliness speaks for itself – and the Common Coral Tree (*Erythrina lysistemon*) whose tempestuous scarlet flowers have their field day on a virtually leafless tree. Coveted lucky beans are the fruit of this tree, nestled in long thin bubbled pods. The basalt soils in the east of this southern region around Lower Sabie Camp are covered in bushwillow and acacia savannah – Knob-thorn (*Acacia nigrescens*) and Delagoa Thorn (*Acacia welwitschii*) in particular.

The Skukuza and Lower Sabie camps are established on river banks that are thickly clustered with tall spreading Natal Mahogany (*Trichilia emetica*), Sycamore Fig (*Ficus sycomorus*) and Sausage Tree (*Kigelia africana*).

Central sector (between Sabie and Olifants/Letaba)

Vast flat grasslands dotted with acacias characterize this well-frequented zone of the Kruger. Mixed in with the knob-thorn

Did you know?

• The spots, stripes or mottled pattern on the coat of every cheetah, zebra and wild dog are highly individual. Each differs from the next one.

• There are few genetically viable populations of wild dog left in Africa; in many packs, all members are related. Lion and hyena prey on 60% of wild dog pups.

• The giant gaping, teeth-baring yawn of a hippo is in fact a warning to intruders not to come too close.

Kruger National Park

acacias and mopane thicket is a dominance of Marula (*Sclerocarya birrea*) as well as Leadwood (*Combretum imberbe*) and Jackalberry (*Diospyros mespiliformis*) trees. The Olifants River, particularly, is lined with Ilala Palms (*Hyphaene natalensis*) and sycamore figs, while further south the Timbavati River is distinctive in its compressed-canopy Umbrella Thorns (*Acacia tortilis*) and Apple-leaf, or Rain Trees (*Lonchocarpus capassa*). Just before the arrival of the summer rains, water forms at the foot of the so-called rain tree, the result of an insect that pierces the bark to suck the tree's sap. In the process the insect discharges an equal amount of water, which drips down the trunk to collect at its base – hence its name. Between September and November, pretty purplish sprays of sweet-scented flowers grace the tree's crown.

The Lebombo hills along the Mozambique border are clothed in knob-thorn and marula bushveld with fronded ilala palms and, on rocky koppies, Lebombo Euphorbias (*Euphorbia confinalis*), straight bare stems topped by a dense, fleshy, candelabra-like mop.

Northern sector (from Olifants to Limpopo)
The much less explored zone of Kruger between the Olifants and Shingwedzi rivers features mainly mopane savannah which increasingly becomes low mopane scrub as a result of the clay soils on chalky calcrete, overlying basalt bedrock. The mopane monotony is broken by various bushwillows such as the Common species (*Combretum collinum*) and red bushwillow, as well as the knob-thorn acacia. The Letaba and Shingwedzi camps are fringed with riverine trees such as ilala, apple-leaf and leadwood.

From the Shingwedzi to the Limpopo in the extreme north, vegetation not experienced elsewhere in Kruger sets this area apart from the rest of the park. Labelled as baobab sandveld and sand forest, tree species include Pod Mahogany (*Afzelia quanzensis*), Sand Camwood (*Baphia massaiensis*) and Red Heart-fruit (*Hymenocardia ulmoides*), whose little nut encircled by a rosy wing is similar to that of some cluster-leafs. The Zulu name for pod mahogany means 'betrothed girl', inspired by the pretty black seeds with their bright red tip contained within flat pods, and alluding to the red head-dress worn by Zulu women before marriage. The sand camwood, from October to January, is

Exploring Kruger sector by sector

covered in delicate white jasmine-scented flowers. Mopane Aloes
(*Aloe littoralis*) stand on tall untidy pedestals, spiky arms crowned
by a branched head of coral flowers, while some gnarled giant
baobabs are estimated to be 4000 years old. Growing along the
eastern border are Ana, or Apple-ring Thorn Trees (*Acacia
albida*) and the Transvaal Mustard Tree (*Salvadora angustifolia*).

Exploring Kruger sector by sector

Kruger is a vast territory with such diverseness in its habitats,
scenery and wildlife distribution that it's necessary to break the park
into manageable chunks to make it easier for visitors to zero in on
the experience they're after. Every sector has its own ambience and
factors giving it specific appeal. Kruger is often criticized for its
extensive network of tarred roads detracting from a true wilderness
feel to wildlife spotting. The park claims the tar allows for better
road maintenance and also, the less dust churned up by countless
wheels, the better it is for the environment. There are also multiple
smaller side roads for visitors to explore, and the further north they
venture, the more wild and untamed the environment becomes.

Kruger's roads are labelled using a code system of letters and
numbers. Tarred major routes linking the main camps are prefixed
with H, then the route number; secondary untarred (but well-
maintained) roads carry the prefix S followed by the route number.

*Below: Bush rangers are
skilled at tracking down elusive
members of the Big Five for
visitors.*

Best Drives –
Southern Sector

• Skukuza–Lower Sabie Road
(H4-1) linking the two camps; the
tight-woven mesh of acacias,
bushveld trees and river-lining forest
hide many of the larger mammals,
including black rhino and the big
cats. Nkuhlu picnic spot offers a
great interlude.

• Nhlowa Road between Lower
Sabie and Crocodile Bridge; the open
plains offer unobstructed loping
grounds to lithe cheetah; also lion
and black rhino.

• Sunset dam, near Lower Sabie,
reminds you of the magic of
Africa – a blood-red orb sinking
in an orange sky as animals slake
their thirst after a hot day.

• Skukuza west along Doispane
Road (S1) to Phabeni gate and the
Albasini Ruins.

• Skukuza northeast along
Tshokwane Road (H1-2) to the
Tshokwane picnic site, taking in the
water holes along the way; lion are
known to frequent this area.

• Pretoriuskop southeast to Malelane
often yields white rhino in the dense
bushveld; look out for Lichtenstein's
hartebeest and sable antelope.

Southern sector (Crocodile to Sabie rivers)

Often spoken of as 'the Circus' zone, Kruger's southern quarter is the most accessible, with five entry gates. What is not contested, though, are concentrations of a great diversity of wildlife – lion, large numbers of white rhino, buffalo, wild dog and spotted hyena are some of the specials lurking in the bushveld.

In general, because a visitor's experience of Kruger is integral with his or her choice and location of camp, a brief description of each camp is included below for all three sectors.

Berg-en-Dal and Malelane: Berg-en-Dal's thatched pitch-roof bungalows of dark and light clinker brick are set on the bank of the Matjulu Spruit in the high rocky hills that give this camp its name. A large-windowed restaurant overlooks a dam. Malelane, offering simple thatched rondavels on the Crocodile River, is a smaller satellite of Berg-en-Dal near one of the entry gates to the reserve. Both are well poised in terms of access to the game-viewing network.

Pretoriuskop: This camp of thatched rondavels on a high-lying plain surrounded by spectacular granite outcrops lies off the mainstream routes, and thus is imbued with a more peaceful aura. The area is good for Lichtenstein's hartebeest, sable antelope and white rhino.

Biyamiti Bush Camp: Self-catering thatched units on the banks of the dry Mbiyamiti River, under sycamore figs and jackalberries, offer a sense of isolation without restaurant and shop facilities.

Crocodile Bridge: Based on the river of the same name and one of the most underrated camp areas, Crocodile Bridge, which consists of thatched rondavels and safari tents, has views onto the red steel of the historic Selati railway bridge. The area is known for white and black rhino.

Lower Sabie: Zinc-roofed bungalows, thatched rondavels and safari tents are ranged alongside the perennial Sabie River under sycamore fig, marula and Natal mahogany trees; a wooden-decked restaurant hangs suspended above the river. Good hippo, elephant and black rhino spotting.

Skukuza Main Camp: If it's frenetic hustle and bustle you want, you have it right here at Kruger's headquarters, a 'mini-village' on the Sabie River bank, with everything from banking,

Central sector

shopping and petrol to a golf course (crocodiles included!). The camp's giant sycamore figs make up for the intrusion of civilization. The Stevenson-Hamilton Memorial Library is crammed with historical artefacts, wildlife displays and enthralling stories, including that of one-time park ranger Harry Wolhuter who was badly mauled by a lion and managed to stab the beast in the chest with his knife. Both lion skin and knife survive to tell the tale.

Central sector (Sabie to Letaba rivers)

Half of the park's lion population – around 60 lion prides – is believed to be concentrated in the great grassy plains of acacia and mopane bushveld occurring in this sector. Elephant, hippo and Nile crocodile love the rivers, and huge herds of ungulates – wildebeest, giraffe, Burchell's zebra, waterbuck and sable antelope – attract predatory lion. Where the king of beasts prowls, wild dogs unfortunately stay away.

Orpen, Tamboti and Maroela: Orpen is a small treed camp of thatched bungalows at one of the park's entry gates. Tamboti is a satellite tented camp on wooden decks under tall tamboti (*Spirostachys africana*) and mahogany trees, while Maroela is a satellite camp on the Timbavati River for caravans and camping only; it has a viewing platform.

Big Five in Birds

Kori Bustard
Saddle-billed Stork
Lappet-faced Vulture
Martial Eagle
Southern Ground Hornbill

Below: Olifants Camp offers pure Africa – azure skies, rustic thatch and views stretching forever across the hot bushveld.

Kruger National Park

• The Nwaswitsontso Loop (S86) and Road (S125) roughly halfway between Skukuza and Satara, where thick riverine forest lining the watercourse gives it its name, offers camouflage to the gorgeously dappled, green-eyed leopard. You have to be stealthy to catch glimpses of this one.

• Satara east to Singita Lebombo concession lodge along the N'wanetsi River (S100) – good for big cats in winter. You are able to get out of your cars at the N'wanetsi picnic site, a great spot against the euphorbia-laced Lebombo hills, to toast the sundown while gazing over the Sweni River and across the flat landscape unfolding to the horizon.

• Olifants south to Singita Lebombo (S90) along the Gudzani Road (S41); keep eyes peeled for the graceful scimitar curve of the sable antelope's horns.

• Satara west, then north to the usually dry Timbavati River (S40) and looping back southward along its course (S39) through belts of sparse-leaved knob-thorn acacia and big-canopied marula trees.

Satara and Balule: From Satara's thatched bungalows and rondavels, arranged in circles around shaded lawns, it's not unusual to hear the deep-throated cough of lion at night. At Balule, a satellite bush camp of simple thatched rondavels lit at night by lanterns, nothing but a low fence separates you from the untamed wilderness. *Roodewal Bush Lodge:* Four intimate low-eaved thatched units in a setting of Natal mahogany and jackalberry trees overlook the Timbavati River; a single booking is required for up to 19 people.

Northern sector (Olifants to Shingwedzi to Limpopo)

The high-lying terrain and spectacular mountain scenery of northern Kruger forms a tract of untrammelled wilderness, distinctive in its fat greasy-grey baobabs and giant sandstone cliffs. It is for those who revel in isolation and solitude, and want to escape the circus of the south. The far north, lying between the Tropic of Capricorn just beyond Mopani Camp and the Luvuvhu and Limpopo rivers, is big beast country, lorded over by heavyweights such as elephant and buffalo, and shared by tsessebe, nyala, and sable and roan antelope. Lichtenstein's hartebeest, which was hunted to extinction by 1886, was reintroduced from Malawi and exists here in small numbers. A long narrow snout and identifying horns that do a Z-like inward swoop make this an interesting animal to train your binoculars on. Careful spotting near Punda Maria could also reward you with sightings of wild dog. The tangled vegetation is lion and leopard habitat, and samango and vervet monkeys scamper through the treetops. The bird life is considered to be the best in Kruger because of the area's proximity to countries further north.

This sector is also distinguished by its heritage of ancient archaeological remains, embodied in the Iron Age site of Masorini Hill near Phalaborwa (west of Letaba) and the Thulamela archaeological site, southeast of Pafuri. The remains of a previous civilization dating to between 1200 and 1640 are evident in the series of loosely packed stone structures at Thulamela, where gold bangles, beads and royal ornaments as well as Indian glass beads and Chinese porcelain were discovered only in 1991. At Masorini, a reconstructed tribal village of thatched wattle-and-mud huts and smelting works provides evidence of a people who lived here in the 18th and 19th centuries. They mined and smelted ore

Northern sector

in ovens to extract the iron, then, higher up the hill, worked the crude iron into spears, picks, axes, and other implements which were traded for grain and other commodities.

Olifants: Often declared Kruger's most picturesque camp, thatched bungalows and rondavels straddle a terrace with 180-degree views over the Olifants River curving away below.
Letaba: Thatched bungalows and safari tents are set in mopane veld on a bend of the Letaba's sandy river bed (Letaba means 'river of sand'); the restaurant overlooks a water hole beyond the fenced boundary which is regularly visited by wildlife. In the Elephant Hall, weighty ivory carried by six of the Magnificent Seven (and other giant tuskers) is on show; there are also 3-D displays and lots more info on this most intelligent and highly sensitive pachyderm.
Mopani: Five stone-and-thatch bungalows perch above the scenic Pioneer dam in this hot bushveld territory and there are great views from the wooden-decked restaurant. South of the camp, visitors can get even closer to nature by overnighting in the Shipandani bird hide, which has fold-down beds and a cooking area.
Shingwedzi: This large complex of thatched bungalows and rondavels, a restaurant, cafeteria and shop is set in a mopane landscape along the Shingwedzi River, close to the Kanniedood dam.
Punda Maria: Thatched bungalows strung along a low hill in the land of the baobabs share this camp with a restaurant, cafeteria, shop and fuel station. It's a zone of sandstone cliffs, rare sand forest and dishevelled 'upside-down trees'.
Boulders Bush Lodge: Thatched A-frame units raised on pillars and linked by elevated wooden walkways nestle into a crop of giant boulders. It's remote and removed from the trappings of civilization; a single booking is required for up to 12 persons.
Pafuri Luxury Camp: This camp is privately owned and run by Wilderness Safaris. Ultraluxurious East African-style tents under thatch sit on a wooden platform linked by wooden walkways, looking out over the Luvuvhu River. Guests can choose to dine under a canopy of majestic ebony trees or under the stars in a *boma*.

Bushveld Camps

Shimuwini: Thatched cottages stand close to the baobab-decorated Letaba River; remote, peaceful with the green Lebombo hills undulating eastward.

Best Drives – Northern Sector

• Letaba, east along the river to Engelhard dam; spot the eyes and nostrils of hippo lurking in the waters! From here (S46) down to the Olifants loop (S44) the route is fringed with leadwood, jackalberry and apple-leaf trees.

• Shingwedzi southeast via Kanniedood dam and hugging the river (S50); vervet monkeys nimbly negotiate the branches of giant sycamore figs, nyala berry and apple-leaf trees.

• Shingwedzi northwest via Mphongolo Loop (S56) along the Mphongolo River to Sirheni; best route of the northern Kruger for buffalo and elephant. Lion and leopard are known to languish in the dense riverine vegetation, from nyala- and jackalberries to apple-leafs and leadwoods.

• Punda Maria directly north to Pafuri gate (H1-8/H1-9), passing massive bouldered sandstone koppies guarded by fat-girthed baobabs; such a big wild landscape demands creatures of equal stature, and brooding buffalo stare balefully from under their heavy bosses while great ghostly shapes of elephant melt into the dense bush savannah.

Kruger National Park

Pafuri Bird Life

Pel's Fishing Owl
Lemon-breasted Canary
Wattle-eyed Flycatcher
Thick-billed Cuckoo
Racket-tailed Roller
Narina Trogon
Böhm's Spinetail

Bateleur: Cottages line the banks of the dry Mashokwe Spruit in bushwillow and mopane woodland; a wooden hide stands at a nearby spot in the river bed which fills with water in summer. *Sirheni:* Cottages are tucked into riverine forest near the dam of the same name on the Mphongolo River; a hide at the perimeter fence overlooks the dam, home to crocs and hippos. Night calls of lion and hyena often colour your dreams, as kills do occur at the water; a supple leopard is a regular visitor to the water's edge.

Into the wilderness (on foot, bike and 4x4)

The magic of the walking trails lies in being able to venture into any of seven wilderness zones that have seen little more than a handful of park rangers – and, well, probably a poacher or two. The impact of humans has been minimal, with limited vehicle tracks established and basic bush-camp structures erected. The three-night ranger-led wilderness trails take you into the heart of the bush with nothing between you and the most untamed of creatures but the rifles slung on your guides' shoulders. Heart-palpitating but positively exhilarating stuff.

Olifants Camp is the only one in Kruger to run three mountain-biking trails through wild but soul-rousingly beautiful scenery; technical in nature, they range from 12km (7 miles) to 24km (15 miles). Four 4x4 routes have been established in different sections of the park, and although they don't focus on tricky obstacle-strewn terrain, they take you into zones normally only penetrated by park staff. Taking four to five hours to negotiate, the game-viewing is worth it. The adventure trails are named Madlabantu (near Pretoriuskop), Mananga (east of Satara), Nonokani (Phalaborwa to Letaba) and Northern Plains.

Seven Wilderness Trails

Bushman trail (San art, rhino)
Wolhuter trail (lion, rhino)
Napi trail (lion, rhino)
Metsimetsi trail (lion, leopard)
Sweni trail (wildlife roundup)
Olifants trail (scenery, wildlife)
Nyalaland trail (scenery, birding)

A panoply of private reserves

Cobbled onto the western border of Kruger's central sector is an array of privately owned game reserves, all of which greatly benefit from the transmigration of wildlife across the national park territory after fences were dismantled along the western boundary. These private reserves vie hotly with one another for the ultimate in luxury in terms of bushveld environs, personal service and sleeping quarters. All offer the services of field guides and trackers who conduct personalized walking trails with

A panoply of private reserves

promises of close encounters with wild animals, and dawn, sunset and night drives in open 4x4 vehicles. The best way for visitors to gauge which of the lodges or tented camps appeals most to their taste is to trawl the excellent websites (see page 49), which have inviting photographs of intimate suites, private decks and plunge pools, and ethnically decorated lounges and dining areas.

Sabi Sands Game Reserve

One of the most well-known private sanctuaries is the Sabi Sands Game Reserve, defined by the Sabie River to the south and traversed by the Sand River. Within its borders is a phalanx of lodge establishments, comprising one self-catering family safari camp and 14 luxury, four exclusive and 15 premier safari lodges.

MalaMala Camp: On the banks of the Sand River in low-lying flat bush country, this camp is well loved and recognized locally and internationally. Thatched, ochre-hued architecture is complemented by animal trophies, bronze sculptures and ethnic art, and a great wooden deck looks onto animals drinking at the Sand River. Dinner, beneath the stars in a reed-enclosed *boma*, is announced to the beat of African drums.

Sabi Sabi Bush Lodge: Situated in the heart of the Sabi Sands with views onto a water hole, the décor of this lodge recreates the

Below: To international visitors, MalaMala is among the more well-known luxury game lodges belonging to the Sabi Sands Game Reserve, although accommodation within most of the private reserves is absolutely outstanding.

Kruger National Park

Above: The distinctive black 'tear marks' of a cheetah, running from the corner of the eye down the sides of the nose to the mouth, absorb sunlight so that it doesn't reflect into the cat's eyes – a unique aid while it streaks after its prey.

ambience of the mid-1900s. African wood sculptures are fashioned from tree trunks, branches and bark collected in the surrounding wilds. Suites with glass-fronted bathrooms open onto panoramic views of the bush and a spa offers heavenly treatments.

Selati Camp: A historical railway theme gives the eight luxury thatched suites of this lodge their charming 19th-century flavour. Spot the collector's pieces in each room after finding your way with the help of shunter's lamps along the paths, and pore over the original steam engine nameplates, signals and other paraphernalia in the lounge. The camp, under spreading acacias lining the Msuthlu River, is located not far from the Selati railway line.

Sabi Sabi Earth Lodge: Labelled the most ecologically sensitive lodge in Africa in terms of its design, it draws its inspiration from the architecture of the Middle Ages where buildings were excavated into the slope of their site. Encroached on by vegetation from every side, the textures, colours and shapes of nature have been harnessed by blending straw, stone and pigment into cement plaster. Natural wood sculptures by artist Geoffrey Armstrong occur throughout. Below ground level, one suite features a sculptural rough-hewn headboard created from a tree and its spreading branches.

Thornybush Reserve

Similarly, Thornybush Reserve has its range of family (four), exclusive (four) and premier (two) luxury lodges. At all of them, lavish personal attention and pampering remain paramount. African tribal dancing counts among the extras that are offered here.

Royal Malewane: This is the flagship of Thornybush Reserve, accommodating a maximum of 16 guests in colonial splendour. Six suites are distinguished by Persian rugs, voluminous antique canopied beds and private viewing decks with plunge pools, while elevated walkways link the suites to the main lodge. VIPs wanting to sneak incognito to the reserve can make use of its helicopters and executive jets. Yes, we all wish … For the genuine monied set, the Royal Suite comes with its own chef, butler and masseuse. Eat your heart out.

The others – a reserve roundup

The utter remoteness of *Manyeleti Game Reserve* – Shangaan for 'place of the stars' – encourages the more adventurous to join

Contact details

a rustic trails camp, where hikers shower under the Southern Cross and dine around a camp fire. **Timbavati Game Reserve** makes sure you commune closely with Nature by means of an overnight wilderness hike or a drive at sparrow's peep to watch the copper sunrise, followed by a high-class breakfast. **Kapama Game Reserve** does things with a difference – it sends willing guests off on a dawn or dusk ramble on elephant-back. **Andover Game Reserve** and **Letaba Ranch** are examples of truly wild, undeveloped areas that are greatly benefiting from Kruger's migratory wildlife trundling down ancient routes again to seek out fresh pastures. At **Klaserie Nature Reserve** you can choose East African style – billowing gauzy nets in safari tents on raised wooden platforms – or a tree-house lodge balanced in the branches. At Ndlopfu, in wild **Umbabat Nature Reserve**, guests report sightings of leopard and lion from the seclusion and comfort of their private decks!

Range of accommodation: bush lodges, bushveld camp cottages, guesthouses, regular, guest and family cottages, bungalows, rondavel/huts, safari tents, camp sites. Gate entry times vary between camps; check websites below.

Contact details

For detailed information and reservation procedures for Kruger National Park visit: www.sanparks.org/parks/kruger. For bookings, central reservations (Pretoria), tel: +27-(0)12-4289111 or e-mail: reservations@sanparks.org

Private concession lodges within Kruger

For details and pictures of the 15 private concessions within the park boundaries, ranging from luxury lodges and spas to tented camps, visit www.krugerpark.co.za/cat/Kruger_National_Park_Private_Lodges.html

Private game reserves

Visit www.krugerpark.co.za or tel: +27-(0)21-4241037 (Siyabona Africa) for all private game reserve queries. This site, run by Siyabona Africa, an authorized tour operator for Kruger National Park, has a comprehensive listing of and direct links to all private reserves on Kruger's western border.

When to Visit

Winter: dry, cooler with temperatures in mid-20s (°C) or low 70s (°F); this is impala rutting season and nesting time for birds of prey; large concentrations of game congregate around water holes. Summer: can be searingly hot with 40°C (104°F) temperatures and oppressive humidity; game give birth to their young, birds are in breeding plumage and migrant species arrive.

Useful Websites

• For Sabi Sands Game Reserve's extensive range of accommodation, visit: www.sabi.krugerpark.co.za
• For Thornybush Reserve's range of accommodation, visit: www.thornybush.krugerpark.co.za
• For Pafuri Camp, visit: www.wilderness-safaris.com

Blyde River Canyon Nature Reserve

Blyde River Canyon Nature Reserve

The Blyde River Canyon is one of South Africa's most enchanting scenic areas. Forming part of the Greater Drakensberg escarpment, it has the drama of gigantic cliffs and ramparts but they have been softened by a brushed-velvet cloak of mountain grassveld and shrubbery, the result of the region's blanketing mists and high rainfall. The escarpment is easily accessed from Kruger, via the Orpen or Paul Kruger gates.

Below: Clear evidence of water's erosive powers resides in the Bourke's Luck Potholes.

The canyon, claimed to be the world's third deepest, underwent the same tortuous buckling and splitting as the main Drakensberg massif when Madagascar and Antarctica split away from Gondwana, but in this instance, the weight of a vast shallow sea covering the eastern part of Southern Africa caused inward tilting of the continent edge. The additional weight of magma intruding the sea floor forced the centre of the basin downward, intensifying the height of the outer rim and creating today's dramatic escarpment. Once this sea, already ancient by the time Gondwana split up, retreated, it left layer upon layer of dolomite and sandstone sediments accumulated over millions of years. Across aeons, Nature's sculpting prowess nimbly worked the softer strata to create the canyon's astounding vistas.

Preserving nature's art

A nature reserve of some 290km² (112 sq miles) was proclaimed to protect these scenic assets, and it

Preserving nature's art

curves for over 50km (30 miles) along the escarpment, initially
beside the Treur River, then meeting and encompassing Blyde
River all the way to the Blydepoort dam and beyond. Treur and
Blyde mean 'sadness' and 'joy' respectively, after the emotions felt
by a Voortrekker party who split up in an effort to find a route to
the sea; at the first river the exploratory party was feared to have
perished, at the second, the two parties were joyfully reunited.

A panoramic route along the escarpment summit, between
Graskop and Blydepoort dam, allows visitors into nature's fantasy
world. First off, just outside reserve bounds, is The Pinnacle, a
free-standing cracked buttress of Black Reef quartzite; next is
God's Window, where awe-inspiring views believed obviously to
be the privilege only of the Supreme Being drop some 700m
(2300ft) into the valley and across the deeply forested canyon as
far as the eyes can see. Then, into the reserve, the Bourke's Luck
Potholes mark the meeting of the Treur and Blyde rivers. Here,
swirling pebble-carrying waters have scooped hollows sometimes
6m (20ft) deep into the red and yellow dolomite rock. Early
prospectors once extracted sizable quanties of gold from here.
Finally, detaching themselves from the far wall of the canyon are
the Three Rondavels, with eroded dolerite walls stained fiery
orange by lichens and vegetated domed quartzite caps. Locals like
to call them the Chief's Wives, particularly since Mapjaneng,
meaning 'chief', rises protectively at their flank.

Blyde River's Forest Birds

Buff-spotted Flufftail
Cinnamon Dove
Barratt's Warbler
Chorister Robin-chat
Brown Scrub Robin
Swee Waxbill
Forest Canary

Activities
A number of multiday trails meander across the reserve, taking in
unsurpassed scenery and penetrating kloofs of indigenous forest,
bringing you into close proximitiy with five of Southern Africa's
six primate species: nocturnal greater and lesser bushbabies,
samango and vervet monkeys, and chacma baboons.

Contact details
Visit www.nature-reserve.co.za/blyde-river-canyon-natural-
preserve.html
For reservations and enquiries: tel: +27-(0)21-4241037
(Siyabona Africa)
Aventura Resorts: tel: +27-(0)15-7955141 or visit
www.aventura.co.za/swadini

MAPUNGUBWE NATIONAL PARK

The public received its first inkling of Mapungubwe's ancient secrets in 1934, after the University of Pretoria announced the findings of father and son Ernst and Jerry van Graan, and a group of intrigued friends. Guided reluctantly by the son of a local tribesperson, they had scaled the top of a small, sheer-walled mountain and discovered tangible evidence of a 1000-year-old royal realm, replete with burial treasures of gold, copper and glass beads.

Decades passed thereafter as archaeological excavations got underway; it was a process marked by hindrances and breaks in continuity, the main obstacle being World War II. A major boost to the Mapungubwe cultural landscape, as it was called at the time, was when UNESCO considered it sufficiently significant to receive World Heritage status in 2003. A year later, a brand-new national park was formed.

Park Statistics

- **National Heritage Site**
- **UNESCO World Heritage Site**
Location: 60km (37 miles) west of Musina; ±230km (145 miles) northwest of Polokwane.
Size: 280km² (110 sq miles).
5-star factor: Archaeological site left by advanced civilization.
Of interest:
- San rock art sites – 150 documented, 450+ newly discovered.
- Ancient dinosaur footprints at Pontdrift, on Limpopo River.
- Sleeping dinosaur fossil (*Massospondylus carinatus*) near Mapungubwe Hill.
- 'Stone tribe' – 85 fossilized termite mounds.

Opposite, top to bottom: The mountain of Mapungubwe, viewed here from land and air, and the baobabs that punctuate the landscape.

Mapungubwe National Park

The Golden Rhino

The only known gold rhinoceros in the world – and certainly the most famous of Mapungubwe's treasures – this sturdy, stubby-legged animal was created of two sheets of finely beaten gold foil believed to have been wrapped around a carved wooden core that has long since decayed. Measuring just 152mm (6in) in length, the foil was tacked onto the wood using minute gold nails, as was the single horn – a cone of gold plate – and a pert, upright tail of solid gold, the end of it engraved with decorative notches to resemble a switch. Two rounded gold nails form the eyes and two tubular ears are pinned to the head with a tiny nail in each ear. As a result of restoration efforts, only one complete rhino exists, alongside two separate torso fragments.

Opposite: The rhino, among certain indigenous tribes, is believed to be a symbol of strength, power and royalty.

An intriguing story

The story goes back to the 1890s, to an eccentric Grahamstown-born adventurer and prospector. Francois Bernhard Lotrie is claimed to have been a guide for David Livingstone. Having spent years roaming the northern bushveld and befriending the local indigenous people, he lived out his last decade, so the story goes, in a cave on Mapungubwe's slopes. Lotrie was reputed to have worn a gold bangle on his wrist until his death in 1917, and rumours ran rife of gold treasures he'd stumbled upon whilst exploring a sacred mountain – although no evidence of a treasure was ever found.

This story was passed on to Ernst van Graan by Lotrie's partially blind African friend, Mowena. Van Graan, in turn, narrated it to his son Jerry, a schoolteacher. During a hunting trip in the area, Jerry, with a few friends, encountered Mowena's hut while searching for a water source, and he graciously served them water in a decorated clay pot, over which he was unusually protective. It piqued Jerry's interest sufficiently for him to return with his friends in late 1932 to investigate. When Mowena refused to lead them to the legendary hill, they succeeded in bribing his son.

The scattering of artefacts they found – stone tools, pot shards and beads – excited them so much, they returned on New Year's Day, 1933, with excavating tools. Their finds – the golden rhino, gold bangles, anklets, beads and nails among much else – were made known to the world after van Graan, in a crisis of conscience, mailed a handful of items to Professor Leo Fouché, head of the University of Pretoria's Department of History. This move heralded a defining point in the cultural history of Southern Africa (see time line opposite).

In mid-June 2000, the Mapungubwe Museum was founded in the Old Arts Building, University of Pretoria. It exhibits all the original archaeological cultural material discovered at K2 and Mapungubwe. The precious metal artefacts rank as the earliest recorded and largest archaeological gold collection in sub-Saharan Africa. Completion of the construction of an on-site museum and cultural interpretation centre at Mapungubwe Hill is planned for 2007, where displays will tell Mapungubwe's story.

An intriguing story

Mapungubwe Time Line

1932 Jerry van Graan and a handful of excavating friends climb to the top of Mapungubwe Hill and find evidence of early habitation.

1 Jan 1933 Return with friends to excavate; discover iron rings; gold, copper and glass beads; gold rhino.

1933 Jerry van Graan mails gold items to his former professor at the Transvaal University College (University of Pretoria today).

1934 Archaeological expedition by the University of Pretoria; the site, Greefswald farm, is secured against looters and treasure seekers.

mid-1930s General Jan Smuts proclaims Greefswald and eight other farms the Dongola National Botanic Reserve.

1934–40 Large-scale general excavations at Greefswald; interrupted by World War II.

1937 First paper published by Professor Leo Fouché, head of the Department of History, University of Pretoria.

1947–48 Dongola reserve disbanded by government due to its geographical and political sensitivity, located as it was on the borders of 3 countries; became military reserve.

1950–70 Detailed study of site's different strata.

1970–95 Radiocarbon dating, analysis of strata chronology and cultural significance; rehabilitation of archaeological diggings.

1990s Reserve known as Limpopo Valley, thereafter Vhembe-Dongola National Park.

1995 Transferral of the site, since 1969 controlled by the SA Defence Force, to SANParks for formation of new national park.

1995 to mid-2000 Restoration, preparation of collections for permanent exhibition to the public; establishment of Mapungubwe Museum, University of Pretoria.

2003 Mapungubwe declared a UNESCO World Heritage Site.

2004 (24 September/ Heritage Day) Mapungubwe opened by SANParks as a new national park.

Mapungubwe National Park

Decorative Objects

Decoration had its place too in the lives of Mapungubwe's people. Clay storage-pot remnants feature diamond-shaped cross-hatching and chevron patterns, there are ivory armbands, gold and copper beads, and in addition to the foreign glass beads, locally fashioned discs of ostrich eggshell and land snail shells. Another indigenous product are the garden roller beads, named for the fat cylindrical shape reminiscent of the iron rollers used on cultivated green lawns. Clay moulds were found together with clay beads, indicating how whole and broken trade glass beads were melted, the molten glass poured into the mould, and once set, the clay broken to release the bead. Stylized clay figurines in human and animal form represent domestic livestock, but there is also a giraffe and a hippo. The human figures, with stumps for the head, arms and legs, often reflect female contours.

Back to the Stone and Late Iron Ages

The critical issue is that, geologically, Mapungubwe is Southern Africa's only landscape to feature such a complete set of successive stages in its early history, as well as providing tangible evidence of cultural traditions. It also forms a historical triangle between Mapungubwe, Great Zimbabwe and the 17th-century Khame ruins near Bulawayo, cultural sites whose influence on African society still exists today.

The area's hundreds of Khoisan rock art sites, and sharp-edged calcite and quartzite stone tools unearthed at Mapungubwe, are evidence of earliest man having lived here – Stone Age nomadic hunter-gatherers, the Khoisan, who used carved bows and poisoned chiselled stone to kill their prey. Thereafter, proof of the Bronze Age (whose origins go back to the Middle East around 4500BCE) having permeated Africa exists in the Swahili-manufactured bronze objects found at Mapungubwe. Site excavations also provided firm confirmation of Late Iron Age inhabitants between 970CE and 1290. This time, honed arrowheads were made of bone and tipped with iron. They were the forerunners, believed to have originated around 500CE, of the Bantu-speaking peoples who gradually migrated southward from the deserts of North Africa, displacing the wandering San. These new groups were agriculturalists and cattle herders, their precious livestock a reflection of their wealth rather than a means of survival. They also lived in more permanent settlements, planting subsistence crops and crafting utensils and decorative artefacts, first of copper and bronze, later of iron.

Demise of a civilization

There are also close parallels with Great Zimbabwe, further north. Although signs of habitation on the Mapungubwe site date back to 970 and Great Zimbabwe is believed to have come into existence from around 1250, the royal dwellings on Mapungubwe Hill were around till 1290 while Great Zimbabwe was abandoned around 1450. This points to the fact that during a specific period, both civilizations lived and practised their craft at the same time. Archaeologists believe that towards the end of the 13th century, a number of factors drove the people of Mapungubwe north to Great Zimbabwe, which in turn was to

Botanical and cultural landscapes

become an enormously powerful trading centre. Preliminary influences could have been an increasing population outgrowing its resources of agricultural land, water, and grazing (geologists confirm that one of the worst droughts in 15,000 years occurred here during the Little Ice Age at the end of the 13th century). This would have led to a decrease in the supply of animal skins and difficulty in obtaining ivory – crucial items for barter with the East Coast and its Indian Ocean foreign traders. The likely theory is that traders turned their focus toward Great Zimbabwe, severing Mapungubwe's critical link with Asia, and forcing its inhabitants to disperse to greener pastures. No signs of violent conflict or massacre have been detected at the site.

The Mapungubwe botanical landscape

The park's vegetation is defined as mopane bushveld with some Kalahari thornveld, and along the Limpopo, stretches of closed-canopy riverine forest. Acacias are predominant with 24 species, among these Fever Trees (*Acacia xanthophloea*) and Ana Trees (*Acacia albida*), the latter recognized by their hard apple-ring pods. The Nyala Berry (*Xanthocercis zambesiaca*) is a dense, large, round-topped tree with small yellow-brown berries, and Leadwoods (*Combretum imberbe*) carry four-winged seed pods that turn brown as they dry. Everyone knows the Common Wild Fig (*Ficus natalensis*), a strangler tree draped with scruffy aerial roots, and the Rock Fig (*Ficus tettensis*) whose roots snake into every rock crevice. There are great-girthed Baobabs (*Adansonia digitata*), copses of tall Ilala Palms (*Hyphaene natalensis*), and spreading Sycamore Figs (*Ficus sycomorus*) grow along the river banks.

The Mapungubwe cultural landscape

The park has an impressive location abutting the shining sinuous loops of the Limpopo, while 1km (½ mile) from the crouching bulk of Mapungubwe Hill is a viewsite giving onto an expansive vista of the meeting of the Limpopo and Shashe rivers. Mapungubwe fringes the borders of three countries: Botswana, Zimbabwe and South Africa. Future plans see it merging with Zimbabwe's Tuli Safari Area and Botswana's Tuli Block to become the Limpopo Transfrontier Conservation Area.

Mapungubwe – Riddles of a Name

There appear to be several derivations for the name Mapungubwe, depending on the cultural tongue consulted to decipher its meaning. According to the national park itself, Dr M Motshekga of the Kara Heritage Institute in Pretoria has translated the name as 'place of the stone of wisdom', alluding obviously to the venerated stone mountain where, once, kings lived. On the other hand, one can't ignore the University of Pretoria's parallels made to the word 'jackal' in Nguni (*mhungubwe*) or in Venda (*punguvhe*), giving us 'place of the jackal'. On another tack entirely is the version given by the Lemba people, who are believed to be of Afro-Asiatic descent, which is 'place where molten rock flowed like liquid', a reference to the ancient art of gold-smelting, perhaps?

Mapungubwe National Park

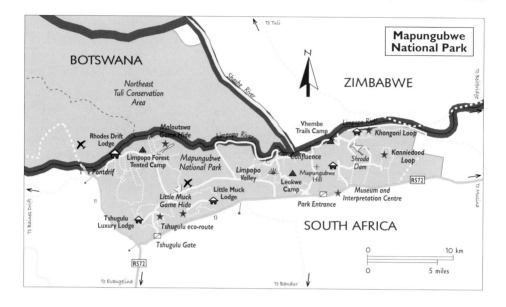

Bird Life

Raptors
Verreaux's (Black) Eagle

Nocturnal
African Barred Owl
White-faced Owl
Scops Owl
Pearl-spotted Owl

Dazzling hues
Red-billed Wood Hoopoe
Crested Barbet
Crimson-breasted Shrike
Meyer's Parrot

Noise-makers
Tropical Boubou
Southern Boubou
Arrow-marked Babbler
Orange-breasted Bush Shrike

Mapungubwe Hill

The park's most distinctive feature is Mapungubwe Hill, a free-standing, sharp-edged, oblong bastion of sandstone and rock cliffs which protects the remnants of a king's settlement. An elongation of 300m (1000ft), it rises 30m (100ft) above a dramatic bouldered landscape, rocky koppies punctuating the bushveld of butterfly-leaved mopanes, wiry acacias and fat grey baobabs.

Three royal graves were discovered on the hill together with the rubble of burnt huts, wall remains, work platforms and grindstones. They were also the only graves to yield decorative gold artefacts – anklets, arm bangles, gold nails, a golden bowl filled to the brim with gold and glass beads, a sceptre, and of course, most famous of all, the 15.2cm (6in) golden rhinoceros. The wealthiest site turned up 2.2kg (5lb) of gold and over 12,000 gold beads.

Radiocarbon dating shows this settlement to be the youngest of the three main excavated areas, pegging its age at between 1220 and 1290. The latter date marks the end of this society in the area. The significance, too, of this mountain refuge is that it's the

Analysis of a lifestyle

first evidence in South Africa of a class hierarchy, where the king physically removed himself from his common subjects, living on high with his royal aides.

Southern Terrace and K2

Archaeologists date the Southern Terrace, lying at the southern foot of Mapungubwe Hill, from 1070 onward, with the oldest site being K2. This lies in a valley on the lee side of Bambandyanalo Hill, which in turn is situated southwest of Mapungubwe. K2, dating from 970–1070, was named by Captain Guy Attwater Gardner, who undertook the early excavations during the 1930s, after North Africa's successive settlements named *koms*.

Analysis of a lifestyle

Seventy years of excavations at all three sites have succeeded in reconstructing the lifestyle of successive generations of a wealthy, technologically advanced society. Settled along the confluence of two rivers, they benefited from a yearly Nile-type flooding that left behind fertile soils for subsistence farming – evident in the terraces and stone walls. Countless clay pot shards containing the charred remains of pearl and bullrush millet, sorghum and beans support this. Unearthed bones show they herded cattle, sheep and goats; domestic dogs were kept too. These peoples were adept as smithies, forging tools, implements and decorative items of iron, copper and gold – the latter washed down by the Shashe River from Zimbabwe's rich ore deposits. Archaeologists found objects such as gold nails, bone, iron and copper blades, iron hoes, and arrow- and spearheads for

Below: The Southern White-faced Scops Owl can be distinguished from the African Scops by its white face-mask framed in black and its bright orange eyes (the African Scops has a grey face and a piercing yellow gaze). Both owl species are the only small owls to have ear tufts.

Mapungubwe National Park

Animal Life

Heavyweights
Elephant
Leopard
Present but rare
White rhino
Lion
Spotted hyena
Brown hyena
Wild dog
Red hartebeest
Antelope
Gemsbok
Eland
Waterbuck
Kudu
Waterborne
Hippopotamus
Crocodile

hunting. Spindle whorls and basket fragments were found, indicating cotton-spinning and basket-weaving, while bone points, awls and flat needles are likely to have been used to sew animal skins for clothing.

Of supreme importance is the role the Mapungubwe people played in bartering with the Swahili traders plying the East Coast. This also afforded them contact with monsoon traders sailing from exotic faraway shores – India, Arabia, Persia, and Southeast Asia. Glass beads known to originate in the Middle East from 2500BCE onward, together with cowrie shells, a known form of currency appearing in lands as distant as China and the Pacific Islands, were discovered in large quantities. Shards of Chinese celadon glazed ceramicware were also found. Foreigners traded such wares for elephant ivory, gold and animal skins.

When to visit
Malaria area. Summer temperatures can rise to 45°C (113°F) but manageable; winters mild with some frost; little rainfall.

Accommodation
Park entrance on Musina-Pondrift road (R572); accessible by sedan vehicles. Hours: 06:00–18:00. No restaurant, shop, petrol station or phones in park. Shops and fuel at Alldays or Musina, 70km (45km) away. All accommodation units fully equipped and self-catering; ceiling fans and/or air conditioning.

Leokwe Camp
The park's main camp; terraced-thatch Venda huts gathered unobtrusively at the foot of bouldered sandstone koppies; swimming pool and bar; 2-bedroom and family cottages, kitchen, reed-walled showers, *lapa*/braai. View site of river confluence and Treetop Hide nearby; wooden boardwalk (with wheelchair access) through treetops culminates in hide overlooking Limpopo.

Limpopo Forest Tented Camp
Wood-and-canvas 2-bed tents and semi-luxury 2-bed tents including kitchen and shower on wooden platforms, sheltered by high forest trees; camp caters for 16 people; facilities for the physically impaired. Close to Maloutswa Pan and hide for great bird-watching and wildlife spotting.

Accommodation and contact details

Tshugulu Luxury Lodge
Six-roomed part-sandstone and thatched lodge for group bookings; among enormous sandstone boulders in wild setting, walking unaccompanied forbidden. Spectacularly sited swimming pool at foot of towering sandstone monolith.

Vhembe Trails Camp
Bush camp for 8 people perched on small ridge at edge of Mapungubwe valley; base for 3-day wilderness trail; 2-person A-framed wood-and-thatch units with toilet/shower, deck overlooking valley. Trail passes the Limpopo and explores nearby Mapungubwe Hill and other archaeological sites.

Contact details
SANParks – tel: +27-(0)12-4289111, e-mail: reservations@sanparks.org official website: www.sanparks.org

Mapungubwe tourism – tel: +27-(0)15-5342014
website: www.mapungubwe.com

Curator, Mapungubwe Museum, University of Pretoria – tel: +27-(0)12-4203146, e-mail: mapmuseum@up.ac.za

Below: Wild dogs love the open grasslands where there is plenty of space to run down their prey; it's also important for them to be near water. The life span of a wild dog in its natural habitat extends to only four to six years, its main predator being lion.

KGALAGADI TRANSFRONTIER NATIONAL PARK

The great, desolate Kalahari desert gets the green light for being the largest continuous stretch of sand in the entire world. It also makes up a whopping 80% of Botswana's land expanse in its 1.2 million km² (roughly 463,000-sq-mile) vastness.

In fact, seven countries share its wide open spaces; besides Botswana, the Kalahari pervades the northern reaches of South Africa, eastern Namibia, parts of Angola, the Democratic Republic of the Congo, Zambia, and a large sector of western Zimbabwe.

The land cutting across South Africa's northwestern finger, which jabs into neighbouring Botswana and then expands eastwards into that country, has existed as a 'peace park' since 1948, hinged on an informal verbal agreement between the two countries. Since the international boundary between South Africa and Botswana consists of the generally dry watercourse of the Nossob River, with no physical barrier in sight, wildlife moved freely across the Kalahari sands of both countries.

Park Statistics

Location: 250km (155 miles) from Upington, Northern Cape.
Size: 52,500km² (20,265 sq miles).
5-star factor: Burnished copper and bronze dunescapes.
Of interest: Black-maned Kalahari lions.

Opposite, top to bottom: The hostile desert environment has bred a hardy, wily people in the Khoisan (centre) – and in its wildlife, with heat-adapting animals such as gemsbok (top) and Kalahari lion (bottom).

Kgalagadi Transfrontier National Park

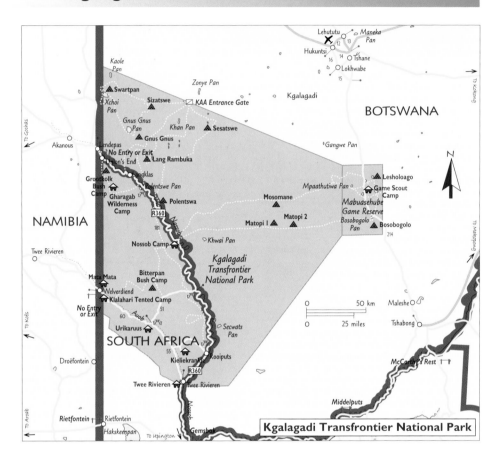

On the South African side, the Kalahari Gemsbok had already been established in 1932 to offer some measure of protection for the elegant gemsbok and also the smaller, daintier springbok, both of which were being killed on a large scale. The peace park encompassed this and Botswana's Gemsbok National Park which, on its extreme eastern boundary, butted onto the rectangular block of Mabuasehube Game Reserve. In 1992, SANParks began negotiations with Botswana's wildlife authorities to manage the entire conservation tract as a single unit. An agreement was signed in 1999, and in May 2000, Africa's first official peace park was launched to the public as the Kgalagadi Transfrontier Park. Almost twice the size of Kruger, its impressive scale makes it one of the select few conservation

Into the desert wilderness

areas of such magnitude left on the globe. The agreement is such that each country is committed to maintaining its own tourist infrastructure, with a focus on involving the severely threatened Khoisan communities living on the park fringes (see panel).

Into the desert wilderness

People who are uncomfortable with solitude, silence and emptiness expanding to every horizon have no place in the Kalahari. It's a desolateness, however, that gets under your skin … stealthily, unnoticed, subtle. The air is pure, intensely dry and, in the heat of summer, suffocating. Midday temperatures in December and January can hit a scorching 40°C (104°F) – that's in the shade. Ground surface temperatures can measure a searing 70°C (158°F)!

It's no wonder this desert landscape, grateful recipient of a meagre 200mm (8in) of life-giving rain each year, is named *kgalagadi* – 'thirstland', or 'land of thirst', in the San tongue. Summer rain, falling mainly between January and April, makes the air hot and steamy. For visitors, the end of the rainy season promises clusters of animals congregating at the replenished water holes. During the rest of the year, the wildlife relies heavily on the many wind-powered (some sources estimate 80) boreholes that have been sunk to tap into underground water. The cooler temperatures of the winter season, between April and September, generally offer a more comfortable travelling experience.

The Kalahari is constantly referred to as a desert in response to its almost complete absence of surface water and its porous sands and grey-white calcite ridges. In Kgalagadi, the broad, generally dry river beds of the Auob and the larger Nossob, spliced at Twee Rivieren, forge their separate ways northward across a desiccated landscape. They are known to flow only once or twice in a hundred years. However, despite its 'desert' designation, the Kalahari is in fact semi-arid savannah. The arrival of the rains nudges the earth into life, and green shoots of sweet nourishing grasses push up through the sands. These become yellowing tufts and mop-head grassy clumps that sparsely cover the undulating dunes and fill the sandy valleys. Olive and khaki

The Khoisan – an Endangered People

The hunter-gatherer San people (or Bushman tribes, as they are also known) are Southern Africa's oldest inhabitants, in earlier times living on plant roots, fruit and honey. They would also stealthily track wild animals, bringing them down with skilfully aimed poisoned arrows. Roughly 2000 years ago, nomadic pastoral peoples – among them the KhoiKhoi – migrated down from the north, encroaching on the San's territories. Over time, there was assimilation between these peoples, and today they are known as the Khoisan. Through climate changes, drought, re-use of land for conservation and tourism, and a loss of hunting territory, they have been forced into a more established pastoral life – a tenuous existence eked out on the fringes of Kgalagadi. In October 2002, 580km² (226 sq miles) of Kgalagadi territory was returned to the San and Mier communities under a contractual park agreement. This stipulates that they can make symbolic and cultural use of the land, which is still run as a conservation area by SANParks, but the San and Mier receive an equal share in the income. It is one of many new moves to balance fast-dwindling habitation territories with vital conservation.

Kgalagadi Transfrontier National Park

green – sometimes, even, a tender luminescent green – join the colour swatch graded white to grey to brown. The overriding image left by Kgalagadi's magic, though, is the row upon row of orange-red sand dunes rippling like a burnished sea. These parallel dunes, in some areas of Kgalagadi reduced to bleached-white sand barriers (in the absence of iron oxides), are the result of wind-blown sand accumulating around obstructions or vegetation and building up into a ridge. As the first ridge becomes vegetated and stable, new ridges form in front of it, and so on, resulting over time in a series of successive, parallel-lying dunes.

Life, a tenacious thing

The pulse for survival is no better illustrated than in the hardy vegetation that has established a firm foothold in the burnt soils of Kgalagadi. Classified as Kalahari dune bushveld, small grasses growing in clumps carry names like Dune Bushman Grass (*Stipagrostis amabilis*), Gha (*Centropodia glauca*) and Giant Three-Awn (*Aristida meridionalis*) – 'awn' referring to the bristled grassheads. Drought-resistant acacias with their protective thorny exterior include the shrubby Grey Camel-thorn (*Acacia haematoxylon*), whose foliage is, well, grey(ish), the regular Camel-thorn (*A. erioloba*) – both these acacias have bright yellow pompom-like flowers – and the False Umbrella Thorn (*A. lüderitzii*), whose flower balls are white. They can also be recognized by their pods; that of the Grey Camel-thorn is long, slender and curved, at times twisted, its texture velvety grey; the Umbrella Thorn's is short, purple-brown and like stiff leather in texture; while the pod of the camel-thorn is fat and curved like a sickle moon, sometimes forming a part-circle, and covered in velvety cream-grey hairs. Also prolific in the area is the Shepherd's Tree (*Boscia albitrunca*), whose Latin name alludes to the distinctive smooth grey-white trunk. Its leaves are particularly nourishing for livestock – so no guesses as to the origin of the tree's common name – and when a branch breaks, new shoots sprout from the damaged area.

Plants have a unique way of adapting tenaciously to the challenges of their environment. The Tsama Melon (*Citrullus lanatus*), Gemsbok Cucumber (*Acanthosicyos naudinianus*) and Wild Cucumber (*Cucumis africanus*) are prime examples, their value defined by the precious water and nutritious food source contained

Bird Life

250+ SPECIES

Raptors
Black Kite
Yellow-billed Kite
Steppe Buzzard
Montagu's Harrier
Pallid Harrier

Nocturnal
Verreaux's (Giant) Eagle Owl
White-faced Owl
African Scops Owl

Showy species
Violet-eared Waxbill
Shaft-tailed Whydah
Rosy-faced Lovebird (rare)

Terrestrial
Kori Bustard
Ludwig's Bustard

In search of silence ... and an animal or two

within for both the Kalahari San and wild animals. A melon seed oil can be extracted from the seeds of the tsama.

In search of silence ... and an animal or two

The park has two well-forged routes tailing the dry sandy watercourses of the Auob and Nossob. Since many of the pumped water holes dot the length of these meandering courses, there's a good chance of encountering animals come to slake their thirst ahead of the fierce onslaught of the sun. Blue wildebeest, especially, favour these watering spots.

Between the long curving V of the two river-routes, which link all the camps like a connecting up of dots, are two cross-routes through the copper dunes. Shortcuts are available between the

The Social Life of Weavers

You won't get too far in the Kalahari bushveld before you chance upon tall, skeletal trees overbearingly weighted with massive, untidy nests of sticks, twigs and grass. Gracing the skyline like overgrown hippie hairdos, their function is insulation against cold and heat. These are the patiently built nests of Sociable Weavers. They consist of large numbers of tunnels opening up into lots of chambers; during warm summer nights only a couple of birds nest together whereas in the icy frosts of winter, four or five may huddle up close. The larger nests can provide protection to colonies of 300 birds. Sociable Weavers' eggs and chicks are preyed on by honey badgers and Cape cobras, and you're likely to see, once in a while, a Pygmy Falcon hovering over the nested trees.

Left: The male Southern Masked Weaver seen here is very similar to the Lesser Masked Weaver, although points of difference are its red eyes (occurring only in males) and the fact that its mask stops at the forehead instead of higher up at the mid-crown, which characterizes the Lesser Masked species.

Kgalagadi Transfrontier National Park

Auob and Nossob – one links Auchterlonie to Kij Kij, the second, further north, connects Kamqua to Dikbaardskolk. Important to note is that travellers crossing the remoter Botswana part of Kgalagadi must be in convoy with at least one other vehicle. Two routes from the Nossob river bed cut across Botswana territory, the first from Nossob Rest Camp to Mabuasehube (170km/105 miles), the second from Kannaguass to Kaa (81km/50 miles).

The tender, juicy grasses emerging after the rains act as a powerful lure to great concentrations of wild animals, but the game also disperses across the rippled desert sands to the replenished seasonal pans. Reports from visitors claim the witnessing of a superb spectacle – cheetahs on the hunt along the Auob river bed, north of Twee Rivieren. The fluid motion of these supple, tautly muscled cats can build to a speed of 112kph (70mph) in open grassland.

Although giraffe in this part of the Kalahari had been shot to extinction by the early 1900s, they were successfully reintroduced in 1990. Leading actor of this desert stage-set, though, is the black-maned Kalahari lion. Estimates peg the number at just under 450 individuals, grouped into around 40 prides. These lion are forced to travel great distances within the park because of the scarcity of their prey, although a greater concentration of pans and higher rainfall in the north ensure healthy numbers of gemsbok, eland and hartebeest. Another example of adaptation to an unforgiving territory, Kalahari lion survive for long periods without water on the much drier and remoter Botswana side by licking the early morning dew from the grass or even their own body hair. Well-trained eyes can often spot these cats lolling in the lower branches of a camel-thorn tree.

Time for life's smaller creatures

The Kalahari is also the place to take some time out to observe the smaller creatures of our world. Look for oversized ears popping up through the short scrub; they'll no doubt belong to the bat-eared fox, with its quirky small pointed face and bushy tail. Dark-eyed suricates, or *meerkats*, are a firm favourite as they scuttle, pause, rise ramrod straight onto little hind legs to quizzically survey the scene, and scuttle off again. Then there are

Time for life's smaller creatures

Left: Springbok get their name from their habit of leaping vertically into the air, sometimes to 10m (33ft) it's claimed, which they do simply out of a joy for life. With the head lowered, they straighten both front and rear legs at the same time while bouncing up and down, a move called 'pronking'.

the utterly endearing ground squirrels, distinguished by their white side stripes and bushy tails. With not a whit of shyness, they sit up on their hind legs to inspect you curiously, or you'll catch them with fluffed-out tail arched like a sunshade over their head to ward off the hot sun.

Although Kgalagadi has an impressive list of bird species (officially 273 at the last count), two-thirds of these are nomadic or migratory, with several rare vagrants. Raptors are prolific, particularly in summer, and for sightings of these the Nossob river bed is the route to stick to. Tawny, Black-breasted Snake, and Bateleur Eagles are common, Martial and Brown Snake Eagles a little more rare. There are kites, buzzards and harriers, and Gabar and Pale Chanting Goshawks with their red-pink eyes and legs. In the depth of starlit nights, you could hear the Rufous-cheeked Nightjar, and sometimes the stirring call of the Pearl-spotted or White-faced Scops Owl. At the camps themselves, yellow-eyed Spotted Eagle Owls, with pointed ear tufts, actually nest here. In the Auob river bed, keep eyes peeled for flashes of blue on the tail and wing-tips and the streaked head of the Striped Kingfisher.

Kgalagadi Transfrontier National Park

When to visit
Summers 40°C+ (104°F+), winter nights drop below 0°C (32°F);
milder months, Apr–Sep, are best for travelling (*see also* page 65).

Accommodation
Rest camps
All have basic food supplies, fuel; only Twee Rivieren offers fresh
meat, eggs, margarine, bread; no fresh fruit and vegetables. Gate
hours vary with seasons, but roughly 06:00–19:30 (summer),
07:30–18:00 (winter). Entry to entire park possible via Twee Rivieren/
Two Rivers border post; no passport necessary if also leaving from
same entry point. Otherwise, crossing from one
country to the other requires a passport.

Twee Rivieren: park's main camp and admin headquarters, on banks
of dry Nossob. Landing strip, restaurant, swimming pool. Natural peb-
ble-walled units with low-slung thatched eaves and angled wood-pole
support beams; chalets or cottages, with living room, equipped
kitchen.

Mata Mata: 2½ hrs from Twee Rivieren, on banks of Auob
bordering Namibia; thorny Kalahari bushveld, surrounded by giant
camel-thorn trees; 5 simple, unprepossessing chalets; equipped
kitchen, patio, braai facilities; also 2 park-homes.

*Right: Twee Rivieren Main
Camp: the 'two rivers' embodied
in the name are the Auob and
the Nossob.*

Accommodation and contact details

Nossob: 3½ hrs from Twee Rivieren, in Nossob's sandy watercourse; pristine white sand and sculpted desert trees; rustic pebbled, thatched buildings. No phone reception. Two-unit guesthouse for 8 people, kitchen, patio, braai facilities. Also cottages with kitchen, patio.

Wilderness camps

Unfenced; tourism assistant on duty at all times.

Kieliekrankie: 4 wooden-poled dune cabins sunk into undulating sea of dunes; equipped kitchen, gas and solar power.

Urikaruus: 2-bed units raised above Auob, nestled among camel-thorn trees.

Kalahari Tented Camp: 3km (2 miles) from Mata Mata; 15 canvas-walled desert tents of wood and sandbags lining a brick-red dune, above water hole in ancient Auob river bed; 1 luxury honeymoon tent; 2-bed and family desert tents; swimming pool.

Bitterpan Bush Camp: set in dunes between Mata Mata and Nossob, accessible only by 4x4; true wilderness, gas and solar heating. Four atmospheric 2-bed reed-and-canvas units elevated on wooden stilts, linked by wooden walkway, overlooking water hole. Expansive dune views from 6m (18ft) lookout tower.

Gharagab Wilderness Camp: accessible only by 2x4 or 4x4; 2-bed raised log cabins with faraway views of dune ridges and thorn trees; equipped kitchen, gas and solar power.

Grootkolk Bush Camp: 6 hrs from Twee Rivieren, 20km (12 miles) from Union's End where South Africa, Botswana and Namibia merge; 4 chalets constructed of sandbags and canvas surrounded by dunes, looking onto water hole; equipped kitchen; gas and solar heating.

Botswana side of park has few facilities; unfenced wilderness camping at Two Rivers near confluence of Auob and Nossob, Rooiputs further north and Polentswa; take own supplies and water.

Contact details

South African side – for reservations, tel: +27-(0)12-4289111
e-mail: reservations@sanparks.org
visit www.sanparks.org/parks/kgalagadi/

Botswana side – contact Botswana Parks and Reserves
tel: +267-3-9180774, e-mail: dwnp@gov.bw

4x4 Desert Trails

Botswana (single direction)
• Mabuasehube Wilderness Trail (155km; 96 miles), starting at Mabuasehube at easternmost point of Kgalagadi park to Nossob; different bird species to dry river course section (Pied Babbler, Three-streaked Tchagra, Bennett's and Bearded Woodpecker, Red-billed Francolin).
• Wilderness Trail (257km/160 miles), starting from Polentsa, north of Nossob Camp.
• Kaa Trail (191km/119 miles), game-viewing route from Kaa (circular), overnight camping.

South Africa
• Leeudril Loop (50km/30 miles), from Twee Rivieren.
• Nossob 4x4 Eco Trail, visitors travel 50–65km (30–40 miles) a day for three days with a guide/vehicle; interpretive stops; wilderness camping in Kalahari dune veld.

uKHAHLAMBA DRAKENSBERG PARK AND GOLDEN GATE HIGHLANDS NATIONAL PARK

Not many people will deny that the great bulwark of the Drakensberg escarpment tops the drama stakes in the South African landscape arena. Shoring up the border with Lesotho, itself a mountain kingdom of note, the Drakensberg marks the big divide between the massive upland plateau of the interior and the humid subtropics of the KwaZulu-Natal coastline for some 250km (155 miles). Literally translated as 'dragon's mountain' from the Dutch-Afrikaans – and pretty apt once you've witnessed its dragon-tooth ridges, eroded cliffs and soaring buttresses – the local Sotho people saw it from another angle. They called it Quathlamba, 'barrier of spears', and this is embodied in the name given to this World Heritage Site today, the uKhahlamba Drakensberg Park. Six wildlife reserves and six state forests combine to make up its great expanse.

The escarpment is generally spoken of in terms of Lower and Upper 'Berg. The gentle, fluid rise and fall of the green-mantled mounds of the Drakensberg foothills, like an emerald apron spread out at the foot of the bastion and presenting an intensely pastoral scene, fall into the Lower 'Berg. The rocky face and heights of the mountain megalith itself comprise the Upper 'Berg.

Park Statistics

• UNESCO World Heritage Site (2000 – cultural and natural)

Location: ±190km (116 miles) from Durban; Sani Pass only access through Drakensberg massif; Underberg main access to southern Drakensberg; Winterton and Bergville main access to central and northern Drakensberg.

Size: 2430km² (940 sq miles).

5-star factor: Stupendous mountain ramparts visible from every aspect; average altitude 3000m (9845ft).

Of interest: Mountain massif is one of the richest natural galleries of San rock art in the world; up to 600 sites of roughly 35,000 individual images.

Opposite, top to bottom:
Faces of the 'Berg: the snow-layered Upper 'Berg, pastoral Lower 'Berg, and a powerful-winged Jackal Buzzard.

uKhahlamba Drakensberg Park

Birds of Prey

Lammergeier (Bearded Vulture)
Cape Vulture
Verreaux's (Black) Eagle
Crowned Eagle
Martial Eagle
Jackal Buzzard
Lanner Falcon
Rock Kestrel

Cooled lava and sandstone sediments

The Drakensberg massif is made up of clearly defined bands of igneous lava deposited on layers of sandstone. The base layer, which characterizes the rolling Natal Midland hills, comprises sandstone, shale and mudstone called the Upper Beaufort Series. Next are Molteno Beds of coarse, glittery blue-grey sandstone, visible in the Lower 'Berg's eroded ledges. These are topped by the Red Beds – you guessed it, reddish-purple shale or mudstone, deposited some 200 million years ago – and fine, soft, creamy Cave Sandstone that resulted in dramatic cliffs and overhangs. Later this arena would become the artistic playground of the San people, who decorated cave walls with their finely executed paintings over thousands of years. When the supercontinent of Gondwana started splitting around 180 million years ago, the parting tectonic plates allowed molten rock to permeate fissures in the earth's crust. These Stormberg Basalts accumulated on top of the sandstones and over aeons were weathered into jagged peaks, sheer cliffs and sharp kloofs; they remain today in the form of the Upper 'Berg.

Today the uKhahlamba Drakensberg Park covers an extensive area; its diverse nature spaces are made more digestible by their loose division into the southern, central and northern Drakensberg. No direct road network connects up the dots nicely between the three sectors, so it involves a number of circuitous detours to get from one to the other. The Sani Pass in the southern Drakensberg is the only gateway across the entire mountain escarpment – and negotiable by nothing other than 4x4.

Southern Drakensberg
Sani Pass

Visitors using Sani Pass to gain access to the uKhahlamba park will need passports to get through the Lesotho/South African border post. It's certainly a dramatic entry into this realm of the dragons. The base of the pass is guarded by the atmospheric thatched complex of the Sani Pass Hotel and Resort, cradled in a tree-feathered nest of eternal green in the Mkhomazana valley, mountains rising almost within touching distance. From here, the sinuous switchbacks of the pass follow the original bridle path that initially snaked up to the crest in 1913, traipsed by only the most sure-footed of Basotho ponies. The first vehicle to attempt this

Southern Drakensberg

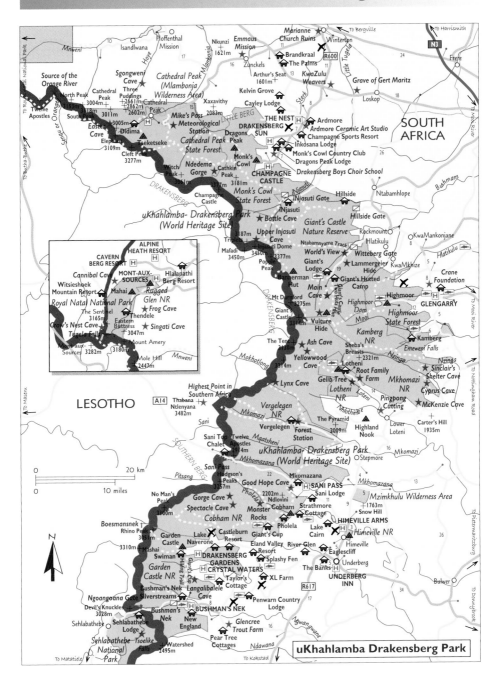

uKhahlamba Drakensberg Park

route only did so in 1948, and the trip took 12 hours. Today, it takes around two, over 22km (13½ miles), with some hair-raising, breathless moments borne out by the names given locally to some of its features – Blind Man's Corner, Haemorrhoid Hill, Suicide Bend and, right at the top, Reverse Corner! The steepest section climbs some 1000m (3280ft) over 10km (6 miles) to the summit, sky-bound at 2873m (9426ft).

Sani Top Chalet poised on the summit has a restaurant and the highest licensed pub in Africa, known for its generous tots (to take the edge off the frosty air); the views, needless to say, are incomparable.

Nearby, carcass remains are put out to the vultures at their very own 'restaurant', attracting fierce-looking Bearded Vultures (Lammergeiers) with their red-rimmed eyes, distinctive black feathers at the base of their beak, russet chest and diamond-shaped tail in flight.

Of hikers and trout fishermen
The southern Drakensberg foothills radiate out like a green velvet shroud punctured regularly by the humps of knuckled hills pushing up under their emerald mantle. The mood is less about the dominating majesty of the northern ramparts and more about the tranquillity of water: cascading falls, trout-filled streams and sheets of mirror-like water reflecting pastoral scenes back to the sky. A contiguous zone of wilderness areas, state forests and nature reserves, it is the dominion of patient anglers and peaceful treed camp sites with mountain backdrops like cardboard cutouts against the skyline. Starting at Bushman's Nek in the south, which is sandwiched between tracts of land making up the Mzimkhulwana Nature Reserve, Garden Castle Nature Reserve and Mzimkhulu Wilderness Area, the southern Drakensberg region curves all the way to Giant's Castle Nature Reserve in the central Drakensberg. At Bushman's Nek is South Africa's only other border post with Lesotho besides the Sani Pass – but it is negotiable on foot and horseback alone. This is also the endpoint of the much-traipsed five-day Giant's Cup Trail which sets off from Sani Pass, tracing the line of the escarpment for just under 70km (43 miles) while crossing the Cobham and Garden Castle state forests.

Southern Drakensberg

Dominating the skyline is the sandstone butte of Garden Castle and, distinctive in its likeness to the profile of a rhino head ending in the upward curve of its horn, Rhino Peak, standing proud of the main range. Look out, too, for The Monk and Sleeping Beauty. A handful of walks includes a challenging eight- to ten-hour hike to the tip of the 'horn', in which walkers gain some 1200m (394ft) in altitude. The last 2km (1 mile) tracks a knife-edge ridge that's to be tackled only in the most perfect of weather, it's so exposed. The 360-degree views are your greatest reward.

Cobham, Vergelegen, Lotheni and Kamberg

All these reserves surround the Mkhomazi Wilderness Area splaying out from the river of the same name. Mkhomazi's remote, under-explored territory features a series of ridges detached from the Drakensberg massif, offering hikers narrow gorges and eroded caves to hunker down in – Cyprus Cave and Sinclair's Shelter afford water and protective night shelter. You could even bump into the area's black wildebeest, eland or smaller, shyer antelope. Otherwise, in the nature reserves, expect undulating grasslands of feathery *Themeda triandra* and dense round-top cushions of Festuca grasses, segueing from apple green to burnished brown and gold depending on the season. Tree ferns flourish along river banks and the creamy yellow heads of the Drakensberg Sugarbush (*Protea dracomontana*) decorate the grassy knolls. Fishermen are drawn to the crystal-watered rivers, trout-stocked dams and mountain lakes – Cobham lays claim to its own Lake District. Hodgson's Peaks, enclosing the Giant's Cup, rear over Cobham while Lotheni's horizon is etched with the unmistakable shapes of The Tent, The Hawk and Redi. If the utter tranquillity of fly-fishing on the Lotheni River (16km/10 miles are stocked with brown trout) is simply too much for you, take a peek into the Lotheni Settlers Museum, an 1890s Victorian homestead once belonging to the Root family. Old wagons, farming implements and household utensils recall a bygone era. Walking trails making the most of mountain views carry names like the Eagle Trail, Jacob's Ladder (a series of stepped cascading falls), the Canyon and the Gelib Tree Trail. Gelib is an acacia grown from North African seed.

The dams in Kamberg Nature Reserve, which is contained to the north by the Mooi River, are replenished with both brown and

San Art's Rosetta Stone

Similar to the way in which the famous Rosetta Stone provided the key to deciphering ancient Egyptian texts, the rock art at the **Game Pass Shelter** gave archaeologists vital clues to a deeper understanding of San symbolism. The site's focal point is a 1.5m-long (5ft) frieze, in red and white tones, depicting eland and humans superimposed. Some of the human figures feature the head of an antelope and hooves instead of feet; they are referred to as therianthropes. Archaeologists realized that here was a spiritual link between human and beast, that hunters – represented as shamans in a trance-like state (also synonymous with 'death') – were taking on the power of the dying animal. These paintings enabled the shamans to share visions they experienced in trance with their San people, and it was the first time that a deeper insight was gained into San cultural beliefs. Other artwork here shows an elephant, blue cranes and figures wearing karosses. The Game Pass Shelter also holds the honour of containing the first San rock paintings to gain attention globally, after they appeared in 1915 in the *Scientific American*.

uKhahlamba Drakensberg Park

rainbow trout, making it a favoured fly-fishing spot – as is the Highmoor State Forest with its high-lying dams, each limited to six anglers. Kamberg has one of the best preserved San rock art sites in the Drakensberg, the Game Pass Shelter (see panel, page 77). Excellent guided trails taking 2½–3 hours are conducted three times a day from the Kamberg Rock Art Centre.

Central Drakensberg
Giant's Castle Nature Reserve, iNjasuti

Tourism is a lot more developed in the central Drakensberg, due mainly to easy access via the N3 highway into the Bushman's River valley and to iNjasuti.

The brooding hulk of the Giant's Castle massif looms protectively over its reserve, the long rugged mountain silhouette resembling, according to park management, the profile of a sleeping giant. Some people refer to it simply as 'the Giant'. You could also try to guess which peak is the Old Woman Grinding Corn, or the Lion, or the Ape. Giant's Castle Nature Reserve was established way back in 1903 to protect the then threatened population of eland and today these weighty antelope number in their thousands, making up one of the country's largest populations. They graze on the grassy slopes of the reserve's battalion of ridge-encircled hills, and their significance in the area is reinforced by their prominence in the San paintings of the Main Caves.

Below: When Scot David Gray and his climbing companion, Royal Engineer Captain Grantham, renamed the prominent Cathkin Peak Champagne Castle, this caused great confusion. Surveyors later restored Cathkin Peak's original name, giving the nearby unnamed peak the title of Champagne Castle.

A half-hour walk from the main camp, an interpretive centre/museum has been created at the Main Caves to elaborate on the four different periods and styles of rock art occurring in the vicinity. Hues for the San paintbrush were derived from mineral oxides: white from zinc, black from manganese, and iron providing ochre through sepia to rust-red. Consisting of two rock

Central and Northern Drakensberg

overhangs, some of the images relate to rain-making, depicting a fanciful elephant, rain serpent and other creatures. Therianthropes, 'flying' antelope and creatures with blood streaming from the nose represent the act of 'dying', often experienced by shamans in a trance state, and symbolize the shamans being transformed in the spirit world into revered eland or other antelope.

From May to September, visitors can join a guided tour (booking essential) to a nearby vulture hide to unobtrusively observe the voracious devouring of meat and bones by not-to-be-trifled-with Lammergeiers.

Four charming stone-and-thatch mountain huts on the Giant's Castle slopes provide shelter for the web of walking trails here, among them a demanding eight-hour round trip from Giant's Hut to 'the Giant's' summit (3314m/10,873ft).

The main contour path here, part of what's called the National Hiking Way, also links the Giant's Castle Camp with that of iNjasuti. This hutted camp takes its name from a river whose translation from the Zulu is, inexplicably, 'well-fed dog' – but the setting is truly spectacular. Human presence is reduced to a mere blip on the radar screen by the staggering size of Champagne Castle and Cathkin Peak, with Monk's Cowl sandwiched in between, which climb into the sky within spitting distance (well ... almost). An 8km (5-mile) circular walk to Van Heyningen's Viewpoint opens up to an unobstructed vista of the Drakensberg rampart, from Cathkin to Giant's Castle.

San paintings at Battle Cave, a four- to five-hour guided walk from iNjasuti camp, feature what appears to be a massive conflict between two rival San clans in addition to a prolific number of other images.

Northern Drakensberg
Champagne Castle, Cathedral Peak, Royal Natal
This region is well served by a road network off the N3; from the main hub of Winterton town, the R600 heads directly into the Champagne valley. In this area, the skyline is blocked by jagged silhouettes belonging to Champagne Castle, Monk's Cowl, Cathkin,

Champagne Castle

The story of Champagne Castle, quite in contrast to champagne air and fairy princesses, concerns two British officers who set out to conquer the peak in the 1860s, a bottle of bubbly snugly tucked into their rucksack. When they stopped to rest, the bottle was discovered to be mysteriously half empty. Loath to blame one another, with the requisite British politeness they mutually agreed to hold the mountain itself responsible for the liquid slippage ...

uKhahlamba Drakensberg Park

Above: Royal Natal's enchanting scenery acts as a magnet to walkers, who can choose from a multitude of hikes of varying length. Waterfalls such as the Cascades, pictured here, can be a mere 15 minutes from the main camp ground.

and Cathedral Peak. Ndedema Gorge, 'place of rolling thunder', enfolds the largest stretch of indigenous forest in the Drakensberg. Backpacking is the occupation of choice here, with a phalanx of evocatively named day and overnight trails. From Cathedral Peak Hotel, a key landmark of the area, one trail offering pure enchantment tracks its way through the yellowwood forests of Rainbow Gorge, where mist from multiple mountain falls is caught by sunlight and transformed into the gorge's namesake rainbows. Giant boulders obstructing the way force hikers to cross the river a few times. Ndedema is also synonymous with well-preserved rock paintings; individual images in Sebaaieni Cave alone top the 1100 mark. For breathtaking views on four wheels, the 10km (6-mile) Mike's Pass starts at the Cathedral Peak camp site and forges to the top of the Little 'Berg near the head of Didima Gorge.

The Drakensberg's most photographed natural feature, the Amphitheatre, dominates the Royal Natal National Park, the northernmost reserve of the uKhahlamba Drakensberg Park. A dramatic 5km (3-mile) curve of solid basalt hemmed in to either side by the Eastern Buttress and the Sentinel, it is part of the Mont-aux-Sources massif where seven streams and rivers start their lives. The Elands (which eventually joins the Vaal), the upper Orange (called Western Khubedu here) and the Tugela are among them. The Tugela pole-vaults over the Amphitheatre's sheer face in a series of earthward bounds; it is credited as being the world's second highest waterfall, next to Venezuela's Angel Falls.

Accommodation

The Royal Natal reserve is a hikers' Shangri-La, with some 25 walks ranging from 3km (2 miles) to the 45km (28-mile) Mont-aux-Sources trail. The superlative Gorge day-walk from Thendele Camp tails and crosses the Tugela to a 60m (65yd) or so tunnel. Hikers can either scramble through the tunnel or skirt it via a chain ladder to emerge in the Amphitheatre, with dramatic views of the curved rock wall, creepy Devil's Tooth and Eastern Buttress. You can also clamber to the summit of the Amphitheatre in a two-hour walk (one way) starting from the Sentinel car park, which marks the end of the road on the northern Drakensberg escarpment; a permit is necessary. Walkers encounter the chain ladders of the Mont-aux-Sources trail, summiting to the same absolutely awesome views.

Anyone tackling the Drakensberg should be aware of sudden weather changes, which can strike at any time, delivering drenching mists, icy clawing winds, and even snowfalls. Always set out fully prepared, and absolutely always sign the camp mountain register before and after your walk.

Car-bound visitors will undoubtedly want to experience the Sentinel Mountain Route, a round trip of some 260km (160 miles) from the Royal Natal National Park, ending at the Sentinel car park. This circuitous road branches out into a wide loop through Oliviershoek Pass, skirting Sterkfontein dam, then doubles back and heads for Witsieshoek Pass toward one of Southern Africa's highest resorts at 2200m (7220ft). The last 5km (3 miles) climbs some 300m (985ft), with stupendous views of the Malutis in Lesotho. Viewsites near the car park reveal the Royal Natal below, the Eastern Buttress, Devil's 'fang' and Inner Tower interrupting the sky at your elbow.

When to Visit

Gate times vary between areas, so check websites, but generally the following applies: summer (Oct–Mar) 05:00–19:00, winter (Apr–Sep) 06:00–18:00;
Royal Natal 06:00–22:00;
Cathedral Peak 24hr gate.
Controlled river trout-fishing season: 1 Mar–30 Jun, 1 Sep–18 Dec; permits necessary. Dams: year-round.
Winter: peaks heavily snow-covered, temperatures icy, particularly at night, but scenery dramatic. Spring/summer: myriad wild flowers, but also spectacular afternoon thunderstorms.

Accommodation
Southern Drakensberg
Garden Castle
Picturesque Hermits Wood camp site in Mlambonja River valley, wedged between Garden Castle Peak and Rhino Peak; no electricity, hot-water ablution facilities; small curio shop with basic groceries nearby.
Cobham
Informal camp sites spread over open area scattered with trees; hot showers; swimming in scenic river below camp.

uKhahlamba Drakensberg Park

Bird Life

Non-raptor club
Black Swift
Alpine Swift
Ground Woodpecker
Orange-breasted Rockjumper
African Rock Pipit
Wailing Cisticola
Lazy Cisticola
Mocking Chat
Buff-streaked Chat
Cape Rock Thrush

Vergelegen NR
Basic overnight camping facilities with solitude and river trout-fishing the focus; within closest hiking distance to Lesotho's Thabana Ntlenyana, highest mountain peak south of Kilimanjaro.

Lotheni NR
• Hutted camp of self-contained chalets, equipped kitchen, fireplace.
• Two self-contained 6-bed cottages with fireplace. Curio shop, Lotheni store for basic provisions.
• Simes rustic cottage beside small, private, trout-stocked dam.
• Mountain view hut looking onto river and mountainscape, for 3 persons; kitchenette (small deep freeze, cutlery, crockery).
• Scenically located camp site, hot-water ablution facilities.

Mkomazi Wilderness
Remote and isolated, the 'Berg's least explored area; 2 caves for overnighting. Cyprus Cave, a 4km (3-mile) hike from wildlife office; for 6 persons. Sinclair's Shelter, a challenging 12km (7½ miles) away across difficult terrain, but rewarding views of Inzinga valley; for 6 persons.

Highmoor
Part of Mkhomazi Wilderness area; limited to 7 tastefully concealed camping sites – the highest-lying in the 'Berg, so very, very cold ... Showers are hot! Feeling of privacy and exclusivity here.

Kamberg
• Kamberg Camp: thatched 6-, 5- and 2-bed chalets, communal lounge; set amid rolling grass-covered knolls, dams and trout-filled streams.
• Stillerus cottage: self-catering for 8 persons.

Sani Top Chalet
Close to Lesotho border post. Built in 1958, sleeps 30 people in simple, rustic accommodation, including 10 backpacker-style dormitory bunks; highest licensed pub in Africa.

Sani Pass Hotel
Reservations: tel +27-(0)33-7021320
e-mail: reservations@sanipasshotel.co.za

Central Drakensberg
Giant's Castle NR
• Giant's Castle Camp: 6-, 4- and 2-bed thatched units under high tree canopies, all with lounge/dining area and fully equipped kitchen; restaurant/pub; curio shop.

Accommodation

• Stone mountain huts located below main escarpment, 3 for 8 persons, 1 for 4 persons and overlooking Meander valley.
• Visits to Lammergeier hide (May–Sep): bookings essential, call camp office (see panel).

iNjasuti

• Hutted camp cradled by two streams in northern section of Giant's Castle area; overriding factor is gigantic proportions of Champagne Castle, Monk's Cowl and Cathkin Peak towering above, positively miniaturizing the camp. Self-contained, fully equipped 4-bed cabins, lounge/dining room, fireplace.
• Scenic camp site, hot-water ablution facilities.

Cathedral Peak

• Didima Luxury Camp: thatched, curved-wall, cave-like units resembling the sail-like architecture of Sydney Opera House, but inspired by San culture; 2-bed luxury chalets, 4-bed cabins, 6-bed bungalow, all set in massive upland scenery with views for Africa. Restaurant, bar, cigar lounge, pool, curio shop.
• Scenic camp site, hot-water ablution facilities.

Monk's Cowl

Camp site, hot-water ablution facilities, laundry facilities, curio shop, tea garden.

Northern Drakensberg

Gate times: 06:00–10:00 all year round.

Royal Natal NP

• Thendele Hutted Camp: thatched self-contained chalets for 2 or 4 persons built into green-clothed hills, each with awesome views onto 5km-long (3 miles) rocky Amphitheatre.
• Two 6-bed cottages, each with a cook.
• Luxury stone-and-thatch 6-bed Thendele Lodge (single group bookings) nestled into hill; every window looks onto Amphitheatre; own cook.
• 2 Thendele camp sites, curio shop with provisions.
• Mahai camp site (large): along Mahai River, magnificent mountain backdrop; modern ablution facilities, hot baths/showers, laundry facilities.
• Rugged Glen camp site (small): secluded, also with modern ablution facilities; horseback trails on offer at nearby stables; the reward is small buck and giant mountainscapes.

Contact Details

All Drakensberg areas:
www.kznwildlife.com/
mountains_dest.htm
KZN Wildlife:
reservations/bookings tel:
+27-(0)33-8451000,
e-mail: info@kznwildlife.com
Garden Castle walks:
www.kznwildlife.com/
gardencastle_wc.htm
Giant's Cup Trail day-by-day
itinerary: www.kznwildlife.com/
cobham_trails.htm
Mkhomazi Wilderness cave
permits: tel: +27-(0)33-2666444
Cobham's trails:
www.kznwildlife.com/cobham_wc.htm
Kamberg Game Pass Shelter trails:
camp tel: +27-(0)33-2637251,
e-mail: kamberg@kznwildlife.com
iNjasuti walks:
www.kznwildlife.com/injisuthi_wc.htm
Giant's Castle Lammergeier visits:
tel: +27-(0)36-3533718
Giant's Castle walks:
www.kznwildlife.com/giants_wc.htm
Royal Natal walks:
www.kznwildlife.com/royal_wc.htm
Mont-aux-Sources overnight
camping: Qwa-Qwa Tourist Officer,
tel: +27-(0)58-7134415.

Golden Gate Highlands National Park

Golden Gate Highlands National Park

Park Statistics

Location: ±140km (90 miles) from Royal Natal; 320km (200 miles) from Johannesburg; 390km (240 miles) from Durban.

Size: 116km² (45 sq miles).

5-star factor: Sculpted sandstone landscape.

Of interest: Wild flowers sprinkled across grasslands in spring; breeding Bald Ibis and Verreaux's (Black) Eagle.

The first reserve in the country to be proclaimed a scenic national park (in 1963). Visitors are ushered in through towering portals of Clarens sandstone – the 'golden gate'. Thirteen per cent of park territory consists of bare eroded rock – layers of sandstone, shale, mudstone and silt laid down some 200 million years ago – and it's these giant cliffs and buttresses that provide Golden Gate's focal point. As the dying rays of the sun each day gild the exposed sandstone, iron oxides glow from amber and bronze to rust-red and copper.

The sandstone uplands of the park, elevated at a height of between 1900m and 2850m (6235–9350ft), are shrouded in a luminescent green grassy mantle in spring and summer. This Highland-Sourveld is not much favoured by wildlife, and the park's antelope use only 40km² (15 sq miles), which means numbers need to be strictly monitored in terms of sustainability. The other dominant vegetation, Festuca and *Themeda triandra* grassveld, turns the entire park into a massive expanse of wheaten-yellow through fawn and cinnamon during autumn and winter months.

Golden Gate Highlands National Park

Sedimentary bands and fossilized eggs

Left: Visitors will have fun deciphering the eroded profiles of Golden Gate's sandstone cliffs. This prominent appendage earned itself the name Gladstone's Nose.

Mid-winter heralds blanketing snow, transforming the rearing rock structures into a monochromatic fantasy land more suited to wizards and dragons.

Sedimentary bands and fossilized eggs

In a similar process to the Drakensberg mountains, sedimentation brought about by centuries of wind and water action has built up the park's rockscape. The base layer, the Molteno Formation, comprising coarse sandstone and khaki-coloured mudstone, is visible in the eastern part of the park. This is overlaid by the reddish-brown mudstone of the Elliot Formation, which in 1978 yielded an enormously exciting find – six fossilized dinosaur eggs, three of which revealed clear outlines of the embryos of the Massospondylus species within them. The eggs, significantly, furnished proof of the evolutionary transition between reptile and bird. This rock layer dates back some 180 million years, to the Upper Triassic Age. Other fossil finds included evidence of canine-toothed animals, and bird-like and crocodile-like dinosaurs.

Topping the Elliot mudstone are very fine yellow sandstone bands belonging to the Clarens Formation, best seen in the Golden Gate and Brandwag rock pillars. The characteristic vertical dark streaks in these eroded cliffs are in fact lichen, which thrives on the rain

Golden Gate Highlands National Park

Animal Life

Black wildebeest
Eland
Blesbok
Springbok
Oribi
Grey rhebok
Mountain reedbuck
Burchell's zebra
Black-backed jackal

water rivulets running down the face. Finally, in line with the nearby Barrier of Spears, a layer of solidified lava caps the sandstone highlands, doggedly resisting erosive forces and leaving behind physical features such as the Mushroom Rocks, Ribbokkop (the park's highest peak) and the quartzite-roofed Cathedral Cave. This 60m-deep (197ft) chamber hollowed out of sandstone by a tributary of the Little Caledon River has a hole punched out of its dome-shaped ceiling; during the rains, the river hurtles through the hole into the cave. A brave wade/swim and shin up a chain ladder has visitors peering in wonderment at its cathedral-like proportions. Walks to Cathedral Cave are suspended from April to September to safeguard the Bald Ibis that breed here. The brightly scarlet pate and savage stabbing beak of this ibis vie with the dramatic livery of its iridescent blue-green back and wings. These big birds share Golden Gate's high clifftops with the same raptor species of the Drakensberg thermals (see Birds of Prey panel, page 74).

Poplars, proteas and pretty amazing views

The Little Caledon River, lined with weeping willows and Lombardy poplars, cuts a verdant swathe right across the centre of the park. Although these trees are alien species, they've been

Right: The blesbok has inherited its name from the Afrikaans word for blaze, 'bles', in deference to the prominent white blaze on its nose and the smattering of white on its forehead. Very similar in colouring to the bontebok, the two antelope are in fact subspecies whose subtle modifications are likely to have resulted from changes in climate – the two exist in different zones of Southern Africa. The blesbok male fiercely protects his females from a rival by snorting, then lowering his head and leaping into the air to clash horns with his opponent.

Accommodation

spared for the tranquil beauty they provide. Otherwise, the
indigenous Oldwood, or Ouhout (*Leucosidea sericea*), is conspicuously
present, clearly recognizable by its rough, flaky, reddish-brown
bark and serrated-edged leaves with silky hairs on the lower face.
This tree inherited its name from its worn, twisted trunks and
branches which look and burn like old rotten wood.

Isolated pockets of woodland protea grow on valley slopes. Look
for the Highveld Protea (*Protea caffra*) which has white outer
bracts with pinkish-white to red centres, Silver Protea (*Protea
roupelliae*) whose single creamy flower head is dipped in colours
grading from silvery pink to deep rose-pink, and Lipped Protea
(*Protea subvestita*), whose outer petals are greenish to pinkish, the
centre creamy white, and the tips of the inner bracts curved back
to form a lip.

There are two short game-viewing drives, Oribi Loop and
Blesbok Loop, with guided night drives arranged from the Golden
Gate Hotel based at Brandwag (the Sentinel). This is an opportunity
to see the smaller nocturnal creatures such as aardwolf, striped
polecat, African wild cat and large-spotted genet. To appreciate
the park's magnificence from even closer quarters, the two-day
30km (18½-mile) Rhebok Trail climbs sandstone heights, traverses
wooded kloofs and fords streams, overnighting in a hut with
water, wood and cooking facilities. The first day notches up 13km
(8 miles), and the second 17km (10½ miles), part of which is a
trek up Generaalskop. In this mountain wilderness, hikers should
be fully prepared for fickle weather.

Accommodation
Golden Gate Hotel: suite, hotel rooms and chalets, restaurant,
pool; resort-type activities.
Glen Reenen Rest Camp: 4-bed thatched rondavels, basically
equipped kitchen; family cottages.
Highlands Mountain Retreat: luxury log cabins on edge of hill;
1 or 2 bedrooms en suite; fireplace.
Noord-Brabant Farmhouse: rustic converted farmhouse for 7
persons, wooden floors and ceilings.
Camping: Shady grounds, communal ablution and kitchen
facilities, barbecue facilities.

Contact Details

For reservations, tel: +27 (O)12-
4289111 (central office) or e-mail:
reservations@sanparks.org
website: www.sanparks.org/parks/
golden_gate

HLUHLUWE-IMFOLOZI NATIONAL PARK

Hluhluwe-
iMfolozi
National Park

INDIAN OCEAN

• Durban

This part of KwaZulu-Natal is infused with centuries of history that span early waves of tribal immigration from the north, inevitable clashes for supremacy, and the explosive battles ensuing as a result. The Hluhluwe-iMfolozi National Park therefore displays a historical richness that is absent in many other reserves.

Indeed it is, together with Lake St Lucia, Africa's oldest established conservation area. Proclaimed in 1895 to protect white rhino from the very serious threat of extinction, the park's orbit was at one time the hunting ground of Mthethwa king Dingiswayo and, later, the famous Zulu king Shaka.

Evidence of Zulu presence in the park can be seen in grinding stones – large indented boulders carrying smoothly eroded 'roller' stones – and enormous depressions dug out of open grassland zones that reportedly served as Shaka's game pits. In earlier days wildlife would be driven into these areas and shot to celebrate a battle victory.

Park Statistics

Location: 270km (168 miles) from Durban; 625km (388 miles) from Johannesburg.
Size: 965km² (370 sq miles).
5-star factor: White rhino conservation.
Of interest: Wilderness walks in truly untamed bushveld.

Opposite, top to bottom: The Black iMfolozi was the focus of intense tribal clashes from the 16th century on; the successful protection of white rhino has gained this national park worldwide fame; their lurid-hued heads make Lappet-faced Vultures fascinating to observe.

Hluhluwe-iMfolozi National Park

Animal Life

Big Five
Elephant
Black (and White) rhino
Buffalo
Lion
Leopard
Carnivores
Cheetah
Wild dog
Spotted hyena
Black-backed jackal
Sideshows
Nyala
Samango monkey

Seat of the mighty Zulu

The area's earliest migrants, the Lala people, who arrived in the 15th century, are believed to have come from the west coast of Africa. Thereafter, from the mid-16th century to the early 19th century, various groups belonging to the northern Nguni peoples migrated to the area: the Zulu clan west of today's iMfolozi border and south of the White iMfolozi River, the Ndwandwe clan along the north bank of the Black iMfolozi, and the Mthethwa between the two rivers. Rivalry and the struggle for supremacy across the decades culminated in the powerful Zulu nation, presided over by Shaka in 1819. After Shaka's death, during the reign of his half-brother, Mpande, hordes of white hunters pervaded the region following 1840, spurred on by the accounts of bountiful wildlife by early hunter-explorers like Frederick Courtney Selous. The marksmanship of both Zulu royalty and avaricious European hunters saw to it that, as the 20th century was ready to be ushered in, many wild animal species were already on the verge of extinction.

Reports give the last sighting of an elephant (prolific up to 1850) somewhere around 1890, white rhino were believed to not even make up 20 in number, and a poacher allegedly struck the last lion down in 1915. It was the volume of public outcry in 1894 – in response to the shooting of six white rhino where the two iMfolozi rivers merged – that brought about the demarcation of two separate protected areas, Hluhluwe Valley and iMfolozi Junction, into 'reserved areas for game' in 1895. They were separated by a corridor of land that acted as a buffer between wildlife and cattle belonging to the local tribespeople in an effort to prevent the spreading of disease.

Disease – a pox on the land

Firmly entwined in the history of these two reserves is the story of disease and the widespread annihilation of both wildlife and domestic stock. From 1898, when a rinderpest epidemic swept through the reserves and across Zululand, right through to 1954 (a period of regular outbreaks of nagana, or sleeping sickness), cattle in the surrounding areas succumbed like flies. Wild game was believed to host the parasite responsible for nagana, which is transmitted via the tsetse fly, so it was inevitable that they'd be

Seat of the mighty Zulu

targeted. Buffer zones were established around the reserves, and any wildlife occurring here was indiscriminately shot. The only animal to be given any respite was the protected white rhino. During this dark time for conservation, iMfolozi lost its reserve status twice, in 1920 and 1932. By 1952, wildebeest and zebra had totally disappeared from iMfolozi, while other antelope species were fast dwindling in number.

The situation was only remedied after various different methods were discovered to rid the area of its tsetse fly populations. Between 1962 and 1989, land to the west and south of iMfolozi was incorporated into the reserve, fences were constructed and the Corridor belt of land gained reserve status, turning the whole into the Hluhluwe-iMfolozi National Park. From this time on, concerted efforts were made to try to restore the intensive damage wreaked on the natural life of the area. Records suggest that a single lion, likely to have migrated from Mozambique, appeared in 1958; others were reintroduced and a healthy

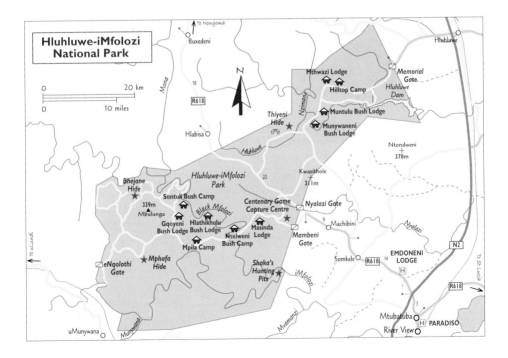

Hluhluwe-iMfolozi National Park

Rhino – Shades of Black and White

The most distinctive difference between the two rhino species is not their colour – which, generally, is the same, varying between different shades of grey – but the shape of their mouths. The white rhino's broad, square-lipped muzzle suits its grazing eating habits; it can often be found standing with its head carried low or cropping short grasses. The term 'white' is believed to have evolved from the Dutch word *wijd* for 'wide', referring to its jaw shape. The black rhino's mouth is long and narrow, with a hooked lip that is adept at grasping leaves and young twigs and manoeuvering them into its mouth. Another distinction of the white rhino is a hump on its neck – absent in the black species – and it has large pointed ears versus the smaller rounder ones on black rhinos. Where calves are present, those belonging to white rhino run ahead of the mother, while young black rhino calves follow behind. Temperament-wise, the black rhino is notorious for its bad-tempered nature and unpredictable behaviour; it's known to charge with little warning – so best keep your distance when in the vicinity of one of these prehistoric-looking creatures!

population exists today although these particular lion are shy and evasive, and therefore not that visible to visitors. Elephant, giraffe, cheetah and wild dog, among others, were all steadily re-introduced into Hluhluwe-iMfolozi.

Benefactor of white rhino

Taking its size into account, the park sustains the largest population of Southern African white rhino in the world – in 2007 numbers were at the 2000 mark. When the park was proclaimed in 1895, there were hardly 50 of these animals still surviving – worldwide. The aggressive protection programme at Hluhluwe-iMfolozi, when the first official survey was undertaken, produced a count of 120 white rhino in 1929. The programme was so successful that by 1960, the existing 700-plus rhino had outgrown their territory. This set in motion the park's highly regarded Operation Rhino, which, after multiple hurdles and setbacks, and much trial and error, has successfully translocated thousands of white rhino to reserves across Southern and East Africa and also the rest of the world. Black rhino share the territory with their white cousins in Hluhluwe-iMfolozi, but in much smaller numbers – the current estimate stands at 250.

In terms of capture methods, the first tranquillizing darts used took 20 minutes to have any effect and by then the rhino had sometimes travelled 8km (5 miles). Drugs were tested and improved and capture techniques refined until the most effective solution was reached – transportation by helicopter. Today, a rhino targeted for capture is darted from a twin-seater helicopter; once it is tranquillized, a Puma helicopter lowers a crew team and crate next to it, the rhino is walked into the crate, after which it is airlifted using ropes and slings to the planned rhino enclosure. Operation Rhino has brought the Natal Parks Board (today KZN Wildlife) worldwide recognition, capped by the fact that the white rhino was the first species to be removed from the IUCN Red Data List.

Visitors can share in the experience at the park's Centenary Game Capture Centre, located in the eastern sector of iMfolozi, near Mambeni Gate. At times animals can be viewed in transit while being kept in holding pens; there are carnivore pens, a

Rivers, hills and grasslands

rhino museum and an info centre that offers audiovisual presentations.

Rampant rivers, forested hills and spreading grasslands

This park of contrasts moves from verdant uplands of tangled indigenous forest and woodland, incised by steep-scarped valleys (in the Hluhluwe sector) to spacious open grassland interspersed with stands of bushveld trees and wiry acacias (in the iMfolozi sector), where, at the fringes, mauve-blue hills rise as a backdrop. Park territory overlaps with the tropical zone in the moist north and straddles the drier, hotter subtropical zone progressing southwards. The preponderance of rivers and smaller tributaries throughout the reserve means that wildlife disperses across the terrain year-round, although the Maphumulu picnic site near Hluhluwe dam and the Sontuli Loop in iMfolozi often yield promising sights of wild animals congregating. Also, in iMfolozi, the sedimentary rock underlying the Mphafa stream's sandy bed promotes more effective water storage, so during brittle winters, game-viewing is generally rewarding at the Mphafa water hole fringing iMfolozi's Wilderness Area.

iMfolozi's two rivers ('black' alluding to the one river's chocolate-coloured pools, 'white' to the light sandy bottom of its counterpart) are capricious and unpredictable. Their catchment area lies distant upcountry, so local weather conditions give no hint as to what's happening upriver. In early 1984, Cyclone Demoina caused an 18m (60ft) rise in river levels, which scoured away entire ribbons of Sycamore Fig (*Sycomorus ficus*) and Weeping Boer-bean (*Schotia brachypetala*), creating extensively denuded river banks that are only fully recovering today.

Special trees to take note of in Hluhluwe's wood and forest pockets begin with the one that gave this part of the park its name. *umHluhluwe* in the Zulu tongue, Thorny Rope (*Dalbergia armata*) in ours, it is a spiky climber, its woody stem winding round and strangling other trees. The Zulu people use the ropey stem to weave muzzles for calves so they can be weaned off their mothers. The Wild Plum (*Harpephyllum caffrum*) is quickly recognizable in indigenous forest by its buttressed straight trunk

Hluhluwe-iMfolozi National Park

of coarse bark topped by a compact crown that's always spattered with red. These scarlet splotches are leaves turning colour, but because they're immediately accompanied by new green ones, there is a constant cycle of leaves ageing and being replaced. The small rosy elongated berries – sour to taste – are relished by baboons, monkeys and bushbabies. Turacos (Louries), Cape Parrots and Bulbuls love to get in on the act too. The Zulu False-thorn (*Albizia suluensis*), with its rounded crown and leaves consisting of multiple stems lined with lots of leaflets, is endemic to northern Zululand only, so conservation is of paramount importance. Samango monkeys chew the leaves and Zulus use the bark for medicinal purposes, specifically to treat the nervous system and reduce fever.

iMfolozi's landscape is coloured by *Themeda triandra* grassland, its reddish-brown grass-heads reaching waist-high in autumn and attracting grazers to its straw-coloured expanse. Thorn trees are scattered across the veld; look out for the Knob-thorn (*Acacia nigrescens*), whose bark is stippled with spine-tipped knobs. In spring, the tree is leafless but covered in pink buds which become cream-yellow flower spikes. You won't miss the Black Monkey-thorn (*Acacia burkei*), the park's largest acacia and, as such, selected by the not insubstantial Black and Lappet-faced Vultures as nesting sites. Umbrella Thorns (*Acacia tortilis*) in turn carry the nests of long-legged Secretary Birds.

The bush experience

Lauded conservationist Dr Ian Player, who was in fact responsible for the implementation of Operation Rhino, was also the first person to establish South Africa's earliest wilderness trails in the iMfolozi area. A substantial parcel of land, defined by the original Parks Board as an 'area of land set aside and managed in such a way that its pristine character is not altered in any way', was identified and all vehicular access to it restricted. Commandeering some 250km² (96 sq miles) – roughly half of iMfolozi's sprawl – only people on foot and horseback may penetrate its savannah thornveld, and impermanent structures in the form of trail camps provide shelter for the night. From mid-March to mid-December, a four-night guided wilderness trail starts out from the Mndindini Base Camp of wooden-poled tented units on the banks of the White iMfolozi River. Two of

The bush experience

the nights are spent deep in the veld with the Milky Way wheeling above, a tented camp supplying the roof overhead for peaceful sweet dreams. Baggage is carried by donkey, while ablutions consist of hot bucket-showers and a spade and tissue roll as toilet facilities!

For pacy city slickers who only have a weekend to unwind, there is a late Friday to Sunday trail, also overnighting at a tented camp, between mid-March and mid-December. iMfolozi has three self-guided foot trails too. Otherwise, two-hour bush walks led by field rangers set off regularly from Hilltop Camp in Hluhluwe and Mpila Camp in iMfolozi. If visitors feel more comfortable on four wheels, the park has three auto trails accompanied by detailed brochures that also analyse ecological aspects of the terrain. In Hluhluwe the three-hour Northern and Southern Auto Trails cover some 43km (27 miles) and in iMfolozi the five-hour Mosaic Auto Trail traverses 67km (42 miles).

When to visit
Summers are hot and steamy with afternoon thunderstorms, so winters (Jun–Oct) are best. Gate times are 05:00–19:00 in summer, 06:00–18:00 in winter. All lodges have cooks in attendance and field rangers to lead visitors on bush walks.

Left: iMfolozi has made wilderness trails a speciality – from weekend excursions for urban types to four-night trail camps.

Hluhluwe-iMfolozi National Park

Accommodation
Hluhluwe sector
Hilltop Camp
• Main rest camp nestled into white stinkwood and wild plum forest belt on hill summit with 180-degree views. Restaurant/pub, lounge, shop, petrol; hide and water hole.

Below: The fact that the thatched complex of Hilltop Camp is the oldest in KwaZulu-Natal belies the luxury of its accommodation facilities. Extensively rebuilt and enlarged in the early 1990s, and the recipient of an international award, it offers options that range from a luxury lodge to appealing self-catering facilities. First prize is its setting on the high summit of a forested hill.

• Luxury thatched Mthwazi Lodge beneath giant sycamore fig; self-catering (with cook) for 8 persons.
• Thatched, ochre-coloured self-catering chalets, communal kitchen and ablution facilities; non-self-catering 2-bed chalets, bar/fridge, tea/coffee facilities. Accommodation for physically disadvantaged.

Muntulu and Munywaneni Bush Lodges
Wood-and-thatch units with reed walls built on stilts on rocky hilltop, linked by wooden walkways; each accommodates 8 persons; individual viewing decks overlooking Hluhluwe River; set in glade of tamboti trees and surrounded by tropical wild date palms. Elephant, rhino and antelope drink at the river, and bushpigs snuffle for figs below the lodges.

Accommodation and Contact Details

iMfolozi sector

Mpila Camp

Painted brick-and-thatch units are spread in an arc on high terrain, pummelled mountains punctuate the hazy purple horizon; self-catering chalets (5 persons); fully equipped cottages (7 persons); single-roomed rest huts with communal kitchen and ablution facilities, braai facilities, cook provided. Curio shop, petrol.

Gqoyeni Bush Lodge

Elevated thatch and reed-walled 2-bed units amongst tamboti and marula trees at confluence of Black iMfolozi and Gqoyeni Stream; wooden walkways lead to central lounge. Booking for single party; self-catering but cook provided. Summer migratory route for elephant, which play on sand banks and reed beds below the lodge.

Masinda Lodge

Thatched main lodge and separate cottage, 9 persons; lounge, dining room, kitchen. Unfenced, overlooking rocky ridges; at times, sounds of lion roaring at night.

Hlathikhulu Bush Lodge

Elevated thatch and reed-walled 2-bed units among tamboti trees; wooden walkways lead to central lounge. Booking for single party; self-catering but cook provided. Resident white rhino; pool created by dolerite dyke across Black iMfolozi harbours hippo and crocodile.

Sontuli and Nselweni Bush Camps

Under tamboti trees overlooking reed beds and sand banks of Black iMfolozi; elevated thatched A-frame two-bed units, central lounge and dining area, fully equipped kitchen, communal ablution facilities.

Contact details

Hluhluwe sector, Main Camp

tel: +27-(0)35-5620848

www.kznwildlife.com/hluhluwe_dest.htm

iMfolozi sector, Main Camp

tel: +27-(0)35-5508476/7 www.kznwildlife.com/umfolozi_dest.htm

General: info@kznwildlife.com

For good images of accommodation (also reservations), visit www.places.co.za/html/1979.html

Marula – Not Only a Cream Liqueur

The Marula (*Sclerocarya birrea*) can be identified by its flaky, patchy bark and, in spring, pinky-purple flower sprays. It is most famous for its fleshy, round autumn berries, appearing from February to June and which turn yellow once they've fallen from the tree. All parts of this tree can be put to beneficial use; besides the fact that cattle and wildlife chew its leaves, bees and insects savour its flower nectar, and monkeys and birds derive great pleasure from its juicy fruit, which reportedly contains four times the vitamin C of oranges. The fruit's stone contains seeds high in protein, and the fruit itself is made by the Zulu people into a potent drink called *ubuGanu*. Stories (whether legend or not) are told of elephant and other wildlife weaving their intoxicated paths through the bushveld after overindulging on overripe, fermenting berries lying on the forest floor. The tree's bark and roots are used, in the form of a hot-water extract, tincture or powder, to treat ailments from fever and ulcers to diarrhoea.

GREATER ST LUCIA WETLAND PARK

The vast watery wilderness of Greater St Lucia – a liquid melding of lagoons, swamps and waterways interspersed with tracts of reeds and papyrus and defined at its fringes by high forested dunes – understandably is South Africa's pride and joy when it comes to pristine wetland areas. Comprising a bewildering array of reserves, each proclaimed separately and managed individually within an integrated unit, the Greater St Lucia Wetland Park begins at the Maphelane Nature Reserve, just south of St Lucia estuary, and cuts a giant swathe north to Kosi Bay, which butts onto the Mozambique border. Encompassed within that great sweep are four wildlife reserves, the country's largest freshwater lake, a coastal forest reserve and a marine sanctuary where South Africa's most thrilling diving experience attracts hordes of scuba and snorkelling fanatics.

Also of great significance is St Lucia's extensive number of biomes – these are classifications of vegetation types into specific habitats, each supporting unique animal and plant life. Ecologists do not always agree on the exact basis of determining each biome, so there are often conflicting reports as to the precise number in this country's protected areas. However, in St Lucia there are clearly at least five of the main biome types (see panel, page 100).

Park Statistics

* UNESCO World Heritage Site
* Two wetlands registered Ramsar sites
Location: 220km (138 miles) north of Durban; 590km (367 miles) from Johannesburg.
Size: 2600km² (1000 sq miles); Mtubatuba main access point to St Lucia's western shores.
5-star factor: Fishing, fishing, fishing! (And scuba diving.)
Of interest: Nesting loggerhead and leatherback turtle guided tours (Jan–Feb); 526 bird species (greatest avifauna diversity in Africa: 50% of South Africa's bird species and 25% of Africa's).

Opposite, top to bottom:
Cape Vidal is one of St Lucia's most pristine slices of coastline; Sodwana's offshore reefs take pride of place as South Africa's diving mecca; hippos lord it over Lake St Lucia's waters.

Greater St Lucia Wetland Park

St Lucia's Biomes

* Mountain
* Forest
* Grassland
* Wetlands (estuary, mangrove)
* Marine and coastal ecosystems
(vegetated dune, sandy beaches,
rocky shores, coral reefs)

A place in the sun for (almost) everyone

The personalities drawn inexorably to this part of the world, like the irresistible pull of metal to magnet, are the fishermen: rock and surf anglers who love the salty sea spray and the squawking of seagulls dipping and planing overhead, or the dawn tranquillity of an undisturbed stretch of estuary or mirror-reflective lagoon, or the sheer thrill of testing their strength at sea against a dorado or bluefin tuna.

Then there are the birding fanatics who come to tick off a great proportion of the 521 species that were officially recorded in October 1998 (now 526 and counting!), when St Lucia was up for its Ramsar nomination (see page 20).

Beyond this, there are simply the naturalists who escape from the crowded summertime fishing and 4x4 fraternity by seeking out the remote, untouched pockets of nature, striking out on any of the large number of hiking and wilderness trails. The wildlife reserves – Mkhuze, Phinda, Tembe and Ndumo – between them have, living on their varied terrain, an impressive line-up, starting with elephant, black and white rhino and the gorgeous big cats, and decreasing steadily in size to vervet and samango monkey, thick-tailed bushbaby and red squirrel. Finally, the waterbabies aim their snorkels, fins and tanks firmly at Sodwana, South Africa's diving mecca, where, it's claimed by some travel writers, the underwater marvels rate on an equal footing with Australia's Great Barrier Reef.

In order to make sense of St Lucia Wetland's vastness, it's necessary to divide it into comprehensible chunks. A good start is the main park's entrance at Mtubatuba, which gives immediate access to St Lucia Village, the estuary and the park's southernmost reaches at Maphelane Nature Reserve.

Lake St Lucia

The village of St Lucia is the commercial little hub of the wetland park. Two excursions of interest that set out from here are the 1½-hour guided cruises on the 80-seater launch *Santa Lucia* and a visit to the St Lucia Crocodile Centre. On the cruises, wraparound views of the estuary from the top deck guarantee plenty of

Pehp cropsnobody

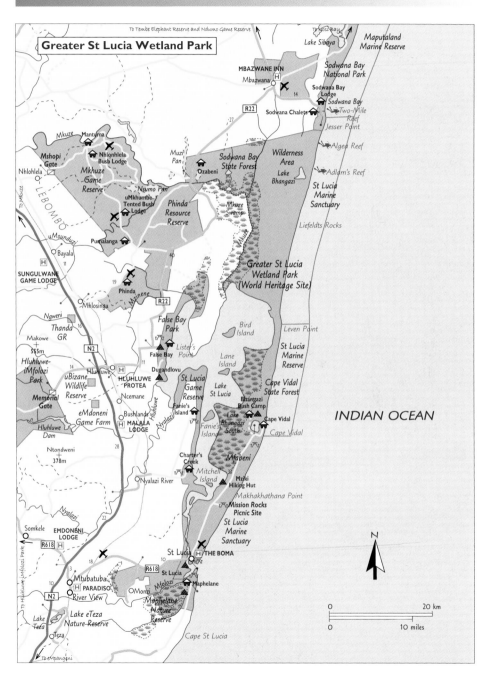

Greater St Lucia Wetland Park

St Lucia Lake

Water Birds
Greater Flamingo
Lesser Flamingo
Goliath Heron
Black-headed Heron
African Fish Eagle
Pied Kingfisher
Giant Kingfisher
Malachite Kingfisher
White Pelican
Yellow-billed Stork
Open-billed Stork
Purple Gallinule
Spoonbill
Jacana
Fish Species
55 freshwater; 212 estuarine
Lake St Lucia
River bream
Yellow-fin bream
Perch
Flat-head mullet
Spotted grunter
Estuarine
Rock salmon
Springer
Kingfish
Shad
Game fishing
Largespot pompano
Barracuda
Sailfish, Bonito
Offshore flyfishing
Kabeljou (kob)
Dorado, Garrick, Shad
Yellow-fin tuna

water-bird-spotting, and the possibility of encountering pods of hippo or the gnarly snout of a croc on a cruise of its own kind. A whole lot more are to be espied at the Crocodile Centre; besides the Nile species are long-snouted and dwarf crocodiles. The best fun can be had at feeding time on Saturday afternoons and, in summer, Wednesday evenings.

The area defined as **St Lucia Park** comprises the strip of land surrounding most of Lake St Lucia, whereas the **Game Park** consists of the entire surface of the water and the islands within it. St Lucia's main lake (around 40km/25 miles in length) empties into the sea via a 21km (13-mile) channel, The Narrows; the estuary is lined with mangrove swamps and casuarinas.

Western Shores

St Lucia's land portion is further defined as the Western and Eastern Shores. The western sliver runs the gamut of savannah, thornveld, sand and coastal forest vegetation. Of the coastal forest trees, White Stinkwood (*Celtis africana*), Wild Plum (*Harpephyllum caffrum*) and Small Knobwood (*Zanthoxylum capense*) can be identified, with perhaps a shy red duiker stepping daintily through.

Falling under the umbrella of Western Shores, the beautiful broad beach of soft white sand at **Maphelane Nature Reserve** has a certain remoteness about it, backed by the tallest forested dunes of the Greater St Lucia Wetland Park – some tower to 200m (656ft). Ten log cabins are built into the dunes, fringed by a profusion of green foliage on the south bank of the iMfolozi River mouth. The decks of some cabins look down onto the activity of 4x4s and ski-boats on the beach sands below, as an offshore reef has created a sheltered bay here, making the launching of boats safe. Rock and surf anglers line the southern bank of the estuary created by the meeting of the iMfolozi and the waters of Lake St Lucia – an inspiring view from the top of the dune behind the camp shows the woven paths of two rivers circumnavigating sandy groves of casuarinas and cutting their beribboned path – finally merged into one – straight into the lazy, slow rollers of the sea. While the fishermen are busy, others can (with the correct permits) go crayfishing, collect mussels off the rocks, explore the

Western Shores

intertidal pools rife with colourful sea creatures, swim at low tide or explore one of the dune forest trails.

Charter's Creek and **Fanie's Island**, both with rustic thatch-rondavel camps settled on Lake St Lucia's shoreline, attract the fishermen, but there are also nature walks for gentle encounters with small buck and antelope, and intriguing bird species with names like Pink Twin-spot and Golden-rumped Tinker Barbet.

False Bay Park is a sliver of land lining the western lake shore and touching the Mzinene River to the north, and the Hluhluwe River to the south. Nature-lovers like to stay at the simple but natural Dugandlovu Camp – open thatched huts partly walled with reed matting – to walk the Dugandlovu (day) and Mpophomeni (3hrs) trails. These pass through grassland interrupted by ilala palms and Silver Terminalia (*Terminalia sericea*) trees, and sand forest of Zulu Podberry (*Dialium schlechteri*) – sometimes called Sherbet Trees – and giant Lebombo Wattle (*Newtonia hildebrandtii*) draped with epiphytic orchids.

Eastern Shores

Sturdy, high-rise, thickly forested dunes composed of Natal Wild Banana (*Strelitzia nicolai*), White Milkwood (*Sideroxylon inerme*), Coast Silver Oak (*Brachylaena discolor*) and Natal Fig (*Ficus*

Above: Protected dune forest, foam-crested breakers and only footprints left behind in the sand at Rocktail Bay ... this is what paraside is all about.

Greater St Lucia Wetland Park

**Coastal Dune
Forest Fauna**

Vervet monkey
Red Duiker
Blue duiker
Bushbuck
Bushpig
Red squirrel
Eastern Shores
Buffalo
Common reedbuck
Western Shores
Nyala
Impala
Warthog
Bushbuck
Bushpig

natalensis) dominate the Eastern Shores, separating the lake's waters from the restless ocean. In between is a puzzle of pans, wetlands and swamp forests. They make up St Lucia's wilderness zone, where very little human interference has left nature pristinely intact. Two guided trails, the three-day Mziki and five-day Emoyeni, explore the wilds around Mfabeni swamp, Tewate Wilderness Area and the shores of Lake St Lucia and Lake Bhangazi, bringing hikers into sometimes close confrontation with animals as thrilling as elephant, black rhino and, just maybe, a glimpse of a leopard. There are also great concentrations of common reedbuck and red duiker – not to mention the hordes of hippo and crocodile that are a permanent fixture in the waters of St Lucia.

Mission Rocks, an exhilarating wind-buffeted, wave-pounded, spray-drenched spot, is a favourite among rock anglers. A nearby lookout point on Mount Tabor has a picnic bench and a toposcope, through which orienting features on the lake can be picked out – Charter's Creek, Fanie's Island and False Bay. Also clearly delineated are the wetland park's contrasting biomes.

An awe-inspiring expanse of light-and-shadow slopes and ridges fills your vision as you enter the barrier dunes of **Cape Vidal**. Once again, this is the domain of shore anglers, salt flyfishermen and sleek, racy game-fishing boats up for the challenge. Offshore, the marine sanctuary begins just south of Cape Vidal and ranges north all the way to Kosi Bay. Here, the waters are clear and crystalline and snorkellers revel in the rainbow spectrum of soft corals and subtropical fish at the offshore Raggie Reef.

St Lucia Marine Reserve extends from just south of Cape Vidal to 11km (7 miles) north of Sodwana's Jesser Point; here, it abuts the **Maputaland Marine Reserve** and stretches to the Mozambique border, forming a continuous protected area stretching for some 150km (90 miles) and 3 nautical miles out to sea. Within this zone are two marine sanctuaries in which no fishing or removal of marine life is permitted – together they are recognized as a wetland of international importance under the Ramsar Convention. A forward-looking conservation proposal is to create, jointly with Mozambique, a Transfrontier Marine

Sodwana Bay

Conservation Area that would extend from Inhaca Island, off Maputo, to Cape St Lucia.

Also demarcating the coast is the protected dune forest of ilala palms, Waterberry Trees (*Syzygium cordatum*), Coastal Red Milkwood (*Mimusops zeyheri*), Natal Mahogany (*Trichilia emetica*) and Lowveld Mangosteen (*Garcinia livingstonei*), promising scintillating sightings of forest bird species. An overnight spot of note is, to the north, Rocktail Bay lodge – steep-pitched-roof units with reeded walls sharing the upper treetops, perched as they are on stilted platforms. This is territory as pristine as you'll get. Nearby, in the crystal waters of Lake Sibaya – South Africa's largest freshwater lake – visitors could come face to face with hippo and crocodile, and they will tick off countless birds from their check lists. A permit is required before driving around the lake.

Sodwana Bay

Its role as a major fishing destination aside, Sodwana's reefs – although not true coral reefs, rather corals attached to sandstone outcrops – lure (it's claimed) 80,000 scuba divers each year. Popular Two-Mile Reef, 12–25m (40–80ft) deep, as well as Five-, Seven- and Nine-Mile reefs keep divers mesmerized with their sponges and soft corals in shades of purple and pink through orange and sunburst yellow. Eerie intricately worked brain and staghorn hard corals, little sea creatures with feather-duster appendages, gaudy sea slugs and bulbous anemones harbouring tiny clownfish all contribute to the underwater panorama. Flitting in among all of this are the reef fish in jewel hues of their own – orange sea goldies, blue-spotted rock cod, pairs of yellow-and-black butterflyfish and aggressive-looking honeycomb moray eels. Out in deeper waters, divers could come face to face with ragged tooth, hammerhead and tiger sharks, as well as whale sharks, manta and eagle rays, dolphins and turtles. They don't call this South Africa's diving mecca for nothing …

Mkhuze Game Reserve

Proclaimed in 1912, this reserve has its fair share of wildlife (three of the Big Five – elephant, black rhino and leopard) but it is more highly revered for its wealth of birds. Besides many of the species visible in the Greater Wetland Park, there's a chance of glimpsing

Coastal Dune Forest Birds

Knysna Turaco (Lourie)
Purple-crested Turaco (Lourie)
Narina Trogon
Twin Greenspot
Eastern Nicator
Yellow-spotted Nicator
White-eared Barbet
Trumpeter Hornbill
Osprey sp.
Grey-headed Gull

Cape Vidal
Narina Trogon
Green Coucal
Brown Scrub Robin
Woodward's Batis
Rudd's Apalis
Yellow-spotted Nicator

Greater St Lucia Wetland Park

Mkhuze's Wildlife

African elephant
Black and White rhino
Leopard
Cheetah
Blue wildebeest
Giraffe
Burchell's zebra
Spotted hyena
Kudu
Nyala

special birds such as Pel's Fishing Owl or Heuglin's and Bearded Robin. The Mkuze River, after cutting through the Lebombo mountains, twists and turns on itself, containing the reserve's northern border. Meandering up from the south is the uMsunduzi River which, together with the Mkuze, feeds a network of swamps and pans – a feature of the park. Generally a flat coastal plain, its tangled wild bushveld is dominated by giant Sycamore Figs (*Ficus sycomorus*) along the rivers, and the pans are lined with Fever Trees (*Acacia xanthophloea*), their sallow hue glowing eerily in early evening light. Two elevated hides in particular, Nsumo and Nhlonhlela, are superb perches from which to spy on the bird life. At Nsumo Pan, prettily decorated with water lilies, the water surface is regularly disturbed by the emerging ears and nostrils of snorting hippos or the menacing snout and yellowed eyes of a crocodile surveying its terrain. Nsumo has also, for many years, been the breeding site of Pink-backed Pelicans – relatively rare in South Africa. Mkhuze's elephant were reintroduced after they were once exterminated in the old Natal by European hunters.

A walk through the sycamore fig forest, with its massive buttressed trunks and great spreading canopies cheek-by-jowl with sulphur-like fever trees, will have you entertained by the echoing cry-baby calls of the Trumpeter Hornbill. Look out for its deep green and white plumage and the large casque on its bill. You might also be assailed by the sweet musky scent of fermenting figs.

Phinda Resource Reserve

This private reserve is contiguous with Mkhuze; it therefore shares the region's five ecosystems and the impressive bird life they sustain. It was an admirable feat, taking extensive effort, to restore it to its original wilderness, since the land was once completely given over to cultivation, and its Zulu name reflects this – *phinda* means 'the return'. Its acacia savannah is home to all of the Big Five, and guests at its four luxury lodges are treated to expertly guided bush walks, birding safaris and dawn or sunset boat cruises on the Mzinene River. With parcels of fever trees, ilala palms, a flood plain, the Mziki Marsh and the southernmost tip of the rocky Lebombo mountains protruding into the reserve, Phinda offers much contrast. Its prized vegetational feature is its 100km^2 (37 sq miles) of sand forest – the largest private stand in the country.

Tembe Elephant Reserve

The best of Phinda's magic, perhaps, lies in its ultraluxury lodges – notably Forest Lodge, set in the sand forest. Glass-walled chalets raised off the forest floor seem to 'float' among the torchwood trees, permitting the secrets of the wilderness to filter in.

Tembe Elephant Reserve

All that separates the two parks in the northernmost reaches of Greater St Lucia Wetlands, Tembe and Ndumo, is a tract of land known as Mbangweni Corridor. Great herds of elephant used to freely tread ancient migratory paths between Mozambique and South Africa until the civil war brought about their decline through major poaching. Of an estimated population of 400 animals, elephant were decimated to such an extent that in 1989 a head count yielded around 120 individuals. Fences were erected along the northern boundary and today Tembe is reputed to be home to KwaZulu-Natal's largest endemic elephant herd. Visitors need to be accompanied by a ranger and day permits are necessary unless you're staying overnight. The dense sand forest – look for False Tamboti, also called Umzithi (*Cleistanthus schlechteri*), Lebombo wattle and Zulu podberry – can provide a very effective camouflage for the wildlife, and you need a sharp trained eye to pick them out. But white and black rhino, buffalo, blue wildebeest and the shy little suni antelope are all there for the spotting.

Below: Cheetah are among the most elusive big cats, but skilled trackers at Phinda are known to reward the luckiest of visitors with a rare sighting of this enigmatic, eternally elegant creature.

Greater St Lucia Wetland Park

Ndumo Game Reserve

The low-lying coastal plain of Ndumo attaches to the Usutu River in the north and is hedged in by the Lebombo foothills to the west. Although Ndumo has the grasslands, sycamore fig forests, and fever trees of Tembe, the most striking aspect of its veld is what's known as 'mahemane' bush – almost impenetrable thickets of acacia and fleshy euphorbias. Again, this is rhino country – no elephant or lion – and the numbers of hippo, and especially crocodiles, are enormous. The pans usually bristle with the prehistoric-looking, sawtooth profiles of crocs lurking evilly on the shores and soaking up the sun. Joining the crocodiles as the park's predatory complement is the spotted hyena.

Ndumo is more reverentially discussed, though, in terms of its spectacular parade of feathered creatures. It is said to sustain 85% of Maputaland's bird species. The Nyamithi Pan is a sure-fire winner for both bird and wildlife watching, and its setting, with a column of luminous waxy fever trees marching along its edge, is positively bewitching. Pel's Fishing Owl, Grey-hooded Kingfisher, Heuglin's Robin and the Stierling's Barred Warbler, with its unusual white chest markings of black bars smudged across its entire chest, are names that don't crop up too often.

Kosi Bay

People who migrate to Kosi Bay's shores love the solitude, footprint-less beaches and absence of sounds bar the soul-stirring call of the African Fish Eagle. They come here to shed their modern, civilized trappings. The name 'bay' belies Kosi's character – it is, in fact, an estuary linking four interconnected lakes that string out southward along the coast. Angling, as usual, absorbs most visitors, including the local Thonga fishermen whose wooden palisade fish traps scar the waters in wavy curves – a distinctive Kosi Bay branding. The lakes, in sequence from north to south, are: Makhawulani, Mpungwini, Nhlange and Amanzimnyama. The latter is fringed with giant-leaved Kosi Palms (*Raphia australis*), whose fleshy fruit and leafy fronds provide food and nesting sites to the rare black-and-white Palm-nut Vulture. Also protected here, in Kosi's coastal forest Nature Reserve, are ilala palms, waterberry trees, Natal Forest Mahogany (*Trichilia dregeana*) and milkwoods – but more importantly, all of South Africa's five mangrove species

Kosi Bay's Mangroves

Indian mangrove (*Ceriops tagal*)
Red mangrove (*Rhizophora mucronata*)
Black mangrove (*Bruguiera gymnorrhiza*)
Onionwood (*Cassipourea gummiflua*)
Springtide mangrove (*Lumnitzera racemosa*)

Accommodation

flourish in the swamps and marshes. This is the only area in the country that they occur together (see panel, page 108).

A guided four-day hiking trail meanders through Kosi's changing land- and seascapes, each time offering night spots set in different scenery while exploring the four lakes, guaranteeing that Kosi's beauty gets firmly under your skin.

Accommodation

Maphelane Nature Reserve
Ten fully equipped log cabins backed into forested dunes; caravan and camp site.

Charter's Creek Camp
Tucked into wooded shoreline, consists of 7-bed cottage, 2-bed self-catering chalet, thatched rondavels with shared lounge and 2 kitchens.

Fanie's Island Camp
Thatched rondavels under coral trees, central kitchen, swimming pool; camp site.

Cape Vidal
Self-catering log cabins at edge of dune forest; communal fully equipped kitchens, bathrooms and communal lounge/dining room; camp site.

Lake Bhangazi Bush Lodge (Cape Vidal)
Four reed-walled, thatched units each with equipped kitchen; five fishing cabins on lake shore.

False Bay Park
Dugandlovu Rest Camp: rustic, very simple thatched structures with reed walls, communal kitchen area, swimming pool, platform overlooking lake; camp site on lake shore.

Sodwana Bay Lodge
Raised thatched reed-walled units against tall dune forest.

Sodwana Bay Camp
Raised, Swiss-style log cabins each with lounge/dining room, kitchen, bathroom; camp site.

Ozabeni (near Sodwana Bay)
Treed camp site overlooking 11 hippo- and croc-filled lakes and pans, northern Lake St Lucia.

Lake Sibaya
No accommodation at present; Mabibi Coastal Camp closed.

Turtle Nesting Time

Although KwaZulu-Natal's seas contain five turtle species – Olive Ridley, hawksbill, green, loggerhead and leatherback – it's the last two that make the most impact on visitors to St Lucia. In summer, between October and March, loggerhead and leatherback females clamber out of the surf at night, laboriously dragging their heavy shells across the sand to the high-tide mark, where they dig a hole to lay 100–120 eggs. Loggerhead eggs hatch in seven weeks (65 days), leatherbacks' in just over 10 weeks (up to 74 days). The tiny, highly vulnerable hatchlings then scurry for the water, under cover of night – but at the mercy of preying ghost crabs. Thereafter, their life in the sea is equally tenuous, with only two in 1000 becoming adults. A monitoring programme in St Lucia tags females and in specific areas notches the hatchlings and checks on these over successive years. Human disturbance endangers these turtles, so driving on beaches is restricted, and completely prohibited between certain hours. Since the presence of humans doesn't deter (or disturb) nesting female turtles at all, fascinating turtle tours are run in December–January.

Greater St Lucia Wetland Park

St Lucia's Ammonites

Intriguing fossilized ammonites the size of small boulders are strewn on St Lucia's Western Shores, along False Bay and also in Mkhuze reserve. They are the remainders of extinct cephalopods which, today, we recognize in the form of octopus, cuttlefish and nautilus. These ancient mud-and-silt moulds of shells that have long since disintegrated date back to the Cretaceous era, 65 million years ago, when major environmental fluctuations caused the ocean to recede. The ammonites failed to adapt to climate change and gradually became extinct during this period. With their coiled, ribbed shell structure, they're believed to be most closely related to our nautilus.

Rocktail Lodge
Near Lake Sibaya, tree-house-style thatched chalets with wooden viewing decks, ceiling fans, shower/toilet facilities separate.

For all reservations, see KZN Wildlife contact details.

Mkhuze Game Reserve
• **Nhlonhlela Bush Lodge:** at edge of Nhlonhlela Pan (at time of writing, dry due to drought), 2-bed en-suite thatched units, central lounge/dining area, fully equipped and staffed kitchen, all connected by wooden boardwalks.
• **Mantuma Main Camp:** consists of 6-bed cottages, self-catering chalets, rest huts with communal kitchen and ablutions, self-catering tented camp; curio shop, pool.
• **uMkhumbe Tented Bush Lodge:** tented (hunting) camp used as bush lodge Nov–Mar; 4 en-suite wooden-decked safari tents, staffed kitchen.

Phinda Resource Reserve
• **Forest lodge:** glass chalets on stilts, hand-built to minimize the impact on rare sand forest; beechwood and slate floors; encroaching forest hides red duiker, suni antelope and rare red squirrel.
• **Vlei lodge:** thatch, teak and glass units on stilts overlooking a wetland system at forest edge, roaming ground of stealthy cheetah; private outdoor deck and plunge pool from which to watch game and bird life.
• **Mountain lodge:** Lebombo mountains provide a blue-washed backdrop for spacious split-level ethnically decorated suites; private decks overlook the reserve; dinner in a reed-and-stone-walled *boma*.
• **Rock lodge:** on edge of rocky cliff, suites of rough-hewn stone and adobe walls with wooden roofs built into rock face overlooking magnificent Leopard Rock; some have outdoor showers, all with private deck and plunge pool.

Tembe Elephant Lodge
Safari camp tucked into sand forest, tents en suite, small pool.

Ndumo Game Reserve
• **Ndumo Wilderness Camp:** luxurious elevated canvas tents

Contact details

with reed walls on Zimbabwe teak decking, overlooking lily-covered Banzi Pan.
• **Hutted camp** of simple thatched rondavels.

Contact details

For all park information, visit KwaZulu-Natal Wildlife's website:
www.kznwildlife.com or www.warthog.co.za/dedt/tourism/maputaland/kznparks/stluciamenu.htm
For accommodation options and images:
www.kznwildlife.com/accommodation.htm
For reservations, tel: +27-(0)33-8451000 or e-mail: webmail@kznwildlife.com

Fanie's Island: tel: +27-(0)35-5501631
Sodwana Bay Lodge: reservations@sodwanabaylodge.com
Phinda Resource Reserve: www.wheretostay.co.za/phinda
Tembe Elephant Reserve: tel: +27-(0)31-2670144
e-mail: info@tembe.co.za website: www.tembe.co.za

Below: Rock Lodge at Phinda is constructed of only natural materials: rock, stone, adobe plaster and wood.

TABLE MOUNTAIN NATIONAL PARK

The uniqueness of this relatively young national park (proclaimed in 1998) is its siting in the midst of sprawling urban development, pockmarked by parcels of privately owned land. Its signature the great looming monolith of that unmistakable mountain, the park follows the rugged rise and fall of Table Mountain sandstone all the way through the tail of the Cape Peninsula to the stormy, wind-buffeted Cape Point.

Holding onto its apron strings is the marine protected area, skirting the coastline from the Mouille Point lighthouse round the apostrophe curl of the Peninsula to Surfers' Corner in Muizenberg, and also extending 10km (6 miles) out to sea. This marine area is estimated to take up some 1000km² (385 sq miles) of adventure playground – and what a playground of contrasts it is.

Park Statistics

• National Monument
• UNESCO Natural World Heritage Site
Location: Cape Town city bowl at the southwestern tip of Africa; encompasses entire Cape Peninsula.
Size: Presently 245km² (95 sq miles); 40km (25 miles) of coastline.
5-star factor: That unmatched flat-topped table that rules Capetonians' lives.
Of interest: New multiday Table Mountain/Peninsula chain hiking trails led by knowledgeable Xhosa guides.

Opposite, top to bottom: Different aspects of Table Mountain: the famed tablecloth, russet-yellow fynbos, and odd-looking (in this case, toothy), furry dassies.

Table Mountain National Park

Kirstenbosch National Botanical Gardens

This giant parcel of estate land bequeathed in 1902 to the public by Cecil John Rhodes does such a marvellous job of preserving and propagating rare indigenous plant species, it's also a World Heritage Site. Only 7% of this beautiful realm on Table Mountain's back slopes is cultivated, leaving a whopping 90% wild and pristine for naturalists, botanists, walkers and hikers. A high glass conservatory has a baobab at its centre, around which all South Africa's floral regions have been recreated, from arid to leafy and wet. Special spaces in the cultivated gardens embrace a herb-scented braille trail, a pocket featuring medicinal shrubs used by *sangomas*, a cycad amphitheatre carrying 28 indigenous species – and for the child in everyone, a magical shady bower of high overhanging trees populated by giant gorilla effigies.

The Cape Peninsula's unparalleled position at the foot of the African continent – although not its southernmost point – exposes it to the influences of two greatly divergent oceans and their currents. The west, Atlantic coastline is brushed by the frosty Benguela current, flowing northwards, whose nutrient-rich waters well up from 300m (985ft) depths in the frigid South Atlantic. In contrast is the southward-flowing, tropical Agulhas current along the east and south Indian Ocean coastline, whose warm waters originate near the equator. There is a tangible temperature difference to the sea on the False Bay beaches as compared with Llandudno, Clifton and Camps Bay, generally attributed to the 'meeting' of these two mighty oceans. In truth, the more likely meeting point is Cape Agulhas, the Southern African continent's most south-reaching point. More intriguing is recent evidence from satellite imagery that shows isolated eddies breaking away from the Agulhas flow, then migrating along the surface of the sea (warming up in the process) into False Bay, bringing with them warmer waters. So, yet another fallacy is shattered: it isn't the meeting of two ocean currents after all.

Of mountain parks and *fynbos*

It's been a tough road for the Table Mountain National Park. Conservationists first raised the idea of a national park in 1929 but in the ensuing years, right up to 1998 when the park was finally established, all that was achieved was Table Mountain being proclaimed a National Monument and the Peninsula's natural areas – 300km^2 (116 sq miles) of conserved land – being declared the Cape

Right: It's easy to see how Capetonians' lives are dominated by the monolithic curve of Table Mountain and adjoining Devil's Peak, on its left flank.

Of mountain parks and *fynbos*

Peninsula Protected Natural Environment. The urban nature of the land and its fragmented ownership caused headaches, but in 1998, the first cohesive reserve structure was established under the reins of SANParks. Today, the Table Mountain National Park encompasses just under 25,000ha (61,775 acres), with the aim of merging the last 5000ha (12,355 acres) of city/state-owned and private land into its preserve boundaries in the future.

An added kudos for the park is the Cape Floral Kingdom – one of only six floral kingdoms in the entire world – sustained by the Cape Peninsula's acidic sandstone soils and across its rocky mountain spine. The Cape's floral kingdom is made up of mainly *fynbos*, a hardy shrub-like vegetation with narrow, finely shaped leathery leaves (hence the Dutch word for 'fine bush') which has adapted admirably to

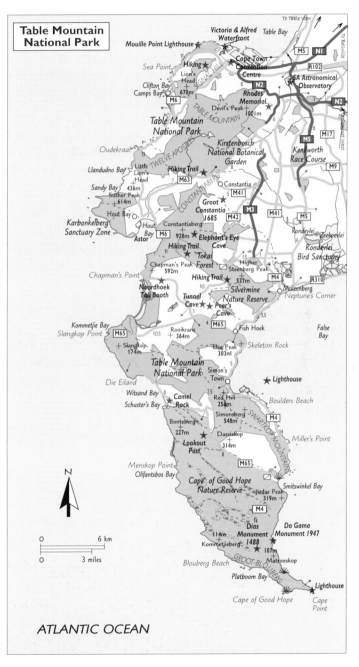

Table Mountain National Park

• The orbit of the Cape Floristic Region (a Natural World Heritage Site) covers the Western and Eastern Cape, from the Groot Winterhoek wilderness through the lofty Swartberg to the Baviaanskloof; 8200 plant species have been recorded here, of which 80% fall into the *fynbos* category.

• Many of the Cape Floral Kingdom's species are endemic – i.e. they are restricted to the Cape, occurring nowhere else on the globe (this is not the case for any of the world's other five floral kingdoms).

• The Cape Peninsula supports over 2285 plant species; 90 species are restricted to the Peninsula only.

• Table Mountain alone nurtures roughly 1500 plant species.

• The British Isles, three and a half times the size of the Cape Floristic Region, has less than 1500 plant species (some 1492 species); New Zealand reportedly has 1996 species.

• The Cape Floristic Region is under threat from urbanization, invasion by alien (or introduced) plant species, wildfires, and pollution and global warming; 29 species are already extinct, 1406 are threatened and 300 endangered.

the shallow, nutrient-poor Table Mountain soils. Among a couple of interesting facts are that *fynbos* relies on fire at least every 15–20 years or so to stimulate a renewed healthy growth. Otherwise it turns 'moribund', meaning it becomes old and woody, allowing healthier plants to take over and in time causing it to die out. On the other hand, if fires flare up too often and burn non-seed-bearing *fynbos*, this leads to sterile soils with a lack of seeds being stored there. The risk is that certain species can be destroyed. *Fynbos*, which in winter and spring produces a gorgeous array of pink-red, rust, and liquid gold to white hues, consists of proteas, heather-like ericas, reed-like restios, daisies and pelargoniums (geraniums). Bulbs, rhizomes and tubers are also part of the family, yielding dainty gladioli, irises, freesias and watsonias. All of which explains why, in 2004, the Cape Floristic Region was declared sufficiently significant to be inducted into the Natural World Heritage Site hall of fame. This status has been applied to eight separate areas within the Western and Eastern Cape, of which Table Mountain National Park (including Kirstenbosch Gardens) is one.

A major threat to the park's *fynbos* heritage is the encroachment of alien vegetation, mainly Australian wattles (hakea), Rooikrans (*Acacia cyclops*), Port Jackson (*Acacia saligna*) and European pine trees, and concerted efforts are being made to remove these species. The same goes for fallow deer, introduced to the Cape by early Dutch and British settlers (and undergoing relocation to other reserves at the time of writing), and Southeast Asian (Himalayan) tahr – the park's feral population was recently killed to enormous public outcry. These wild mountain goats escaped from the former zoo on the slopes of Devil's Peak. Prolific breeding among the fallow deer outgrew territorial bounds and was posing a serious threat to indigenous vegetation. Despite the clamour of dissenting voices, the earliest areas to have been cleared of alien plants are showing remarkable recovery in terms of the original *fynbos* presence. This mountain national park also features belts of evergreen forest in the sheltered ravines and mist-and-rain-fed kloofs along the east-facing scarps of the Peninsula chain.

Moulded by ice and molten lava

One cannot gaze at the hulk of Cape Town's flat-topped mountain without wondering in awe how it came to loom so weighty and

Moulded by ice and molten lava

large over the city bowl. So for those aspiring geologists, here's something to marvel at: its oldest rock strata date back to sedimentation that took place some 550 million years ago. The entire Peninsula chain is constructed of three main rock layers, the lowest being the Malmesbury Group (aged roughly 540 million years) of dark grey mudstone and lighter sandstone. Devil's Peak, Signal Hill and the city bowl are founded on this rock.

Next is a layer of hard, coarse-grained Cape Peninsula granite (540 million years), a composite of white feldspar crystals, glassy quartz and flaky reflective black mica. This forms the main base of the Peninsula mountain chain and also Lion's Head.

It is topped by a combination-layer of Peninsula Formation sandstone on Graafwater Formation sandstone, both part of the Table Mountain Group (520 million years). The Graafwater rocks are recognized by their reddish-purple colour derived from iron oxides, the Peninsula rocks by their grey, pebbly structure and they are the ones that mainly go into the table-top bulk we love so well. The third layer of the Table Mountain Group of sandstones is the Pakhuis Formation, angular pebbles and boulders that were deposited when glaciers were once part of a frozen landscape here; these pebbles are visible on the highest points of Table Mountain, for example, at Maclear's Beacon.

Way back in the mists of time, the entire Cape Province and Namibia were pieces in the puzzle of a gigantic, deep sea-floor beneath an ancient sea known as the Adamastor Ocean (see

Peninsula Facts

* 60 million years ago, between ice ages, rising temperatures caused the ice to melt and sea levels rose by 150m (490ft). What is today the Cape Flats was totally submerged, and all that remained of the Peninsula was a number of islands. This is why a layer of dune and beach sands covers almost half of the Cape Peninsula.

* In 1652 the sea line skirted the grounds of the Castle, at that time a wood-and-cement fort built by Jan van Riebeeck of the Dutch East India Company. In recent times, land was reclaimed from the sea to create today's Foreshore area to accommodate a rapidly expanding city.

* The rubble from the infamous apartheid era demolition of District Six, when people of colour were forcibly removed from their homes and resettled on the Cape Flats, now lines the Duncan and Ben Schoeman docks in the V&A Waterfront.

Left: This much-published view of 'the Table' has drawn thousands to the seaside suburb of Bloubergstrand (literally meaning 'blue mountain beach').

Table Mountain National Park

Animal Life

On Table Mountain
Klipspringer, Steenbok
Grysbok, Grey rhebok
Common duiker
Cape of Good Hope
Cape mountain zebra
Red hartebeest
Eland, Bontebok
Cape Peninsula
Chacma baboon
Rock hyrax (Dassie)
Harbours
Cape fur seal
Boulders Beach
African (Jackass) penguin

Bird Life

Nectar-lovers
Cape Sugarbird
Orange-breasted Sunbird
Malachite Sunbird
Cormorants
Cape Cormorant
Bank Cormorant
Crowned Cormorant
White-breasted Cormorant
Seagulls
Kelp Seagull
Hartlaub's Seagull
Grey-headed Seagull
Protected
African Black Oystercatcher

Legends below). It was at this time that cycles of sedimentation took place, laying the base for today's rock structures. When, around 350 million years ago, the continental plates of South America and Africa collided, massive buckling of the Malmesbury sandstone strata crushed them into today's Cape Fold mountain structure. The contorted and folded sandstone layers can be seen in many areas around the Peninsula where erosion has worn away banks and cliffs.

Table Mountain legends and myths

Stories passed down orally amongst the Cape's earliest peoples and also written records propose Table Mountain's profile as that of a great sleeping giant. Depending on the source, though, he was both malevolent rogue and powerful protector. And Adamastor was not only an ancient ocean – in Greek mythology, Adamastor was also a Titan, progeny of earth goddess Gaea (Gaia) and sky god Uranus. The Titans spread much evil, ruling the earth ruthlessly, and when they were overpowered by Zeus, were banished to the furthest corners of Earth. This is where 16th-century Portuguese poet Luís Vaz de Camões takes up the story; according to him, fierce Adamastor, in the supine form of Table Mountain, jealously dominated the southern corner of the Earth – fending off first Bartolomeu Dias, later Vasco da Gama – with his wild sea-storms. Dias and da Gama eventually succeeded in thwarting the giant, da Gama rounding the Cape in 1497 and making it all the way to India. If you drive into Cape Town via the N2, using a little imagination you can make out the stone profile of Adamastor, Devil's Peak forming his head while his sleeping form stretches southward along the back table ending at the Constantiaberg.

Zulu sage Credo Mutwa, though, retells the ancient story surrounding big-hearted protector Umlindi Wemingizimu, 'watcher of the south'. In this version, the union of sun god Tixo and earth goddess Djobela produced Qamata. Subsequently, Qamata's efforts to create the world saw him battle the great dragon of the sea, who was preventing him from forming dry land, so the earth goddess Djobela fashioned four gigantic beings to protect each of Earth's corners. Countless fierce conflicts later, the giants were eventually turned to stone – permanent symbols of their protective clout. Table Mountain is, of course, the giant of the Earth's southern corner, Umlindi Wemingizimu.

A highly unique Peninsula trail

Since the Khoisan were the earliest people to penetrate the mystique of Cape Town's sandstone bastion, it's quite apt that their name for the mountain and its extended curvy spine – Hoerikwaggo (translated as 'mountains in the sea') – has been given to a new series of Peninsula hiking trails. These offer the best way to absorb nature's wild beauty and gain a seagull's perspective on the lie of the land – which does get confusing, what with a north-facing table, a southeast-curving peninsula, false bays and warm- and cold-water shorelines.

The first of these trails, the three-day Table Mountain trail (25.5km/ 16 miles), starts with a harbour boat trip to get the early seafarers' impression of the southwestern tip of Africa. Next, visitors trawl historic parts of the city via a Slave Trail – the Malay Quarter's flat-topped homes painted in peppermint-pastel shades, the Grand Parade, District Six Museum – ending the day at the foot of the mountain, in Deer Park. Here they sleep in restored washhouses (dating back to 1888) where slave women once scrubbed their Dutch masters' clothes, and dine on fragrantly spiced Malay dishes. Next day, they hitch a ride via the cableway (inclement weather may mean a trek up Platteklip gorge), exploring the length of the *fynbos*-strewn mountaintop and its dams, focusing on Nature's finer details with the help of Xhosa-clicking guides. The night is spent in a restored stone Overseer's Cottage, from the wooden deck of which the city's myriad pinpricks of lights spread out below like a

Peninsula Facts

• The Twelve Apostles were once a fused, contiguous part of Table Mountain – until Africa and South America split away from one another, causing tension fractures in the granite and sandstone. At the mercy of elemental forces, dissolving water eroded decomposing rock, etching out sharp kloofs that have modelled today's familiar serrated profile of the Apostles.

• Peer's Cave in the Silvermine Reserve above Kalk Bay and Fish Hoek is where the skeletal remains of the 12,000-year-old Fish Hoek Man were discovered, together with stone fragments and evidence of nine other individuals, and also bone fragments belonging to the extinct Cape horse and buffalo.

Left: A number of newly established trails across the top of Table Mountain and along its mountainous spine to Cape Point offer visitors and locals alike a novel hiking experience.

Table Mountain National Park

Right: This state-of-the-art Swiss-designed cable car has a rotating floor that turns 360° on its swift glide to the top of Table Mountain.

An Adrenaline Fix by Rock and Air

Rock

Traditional climbing
Table Mountain
Twelve Apostles
Lion's Head
Silvermine
Muizenberg Crags

Sport climbing
Kalk Bay
Silvermine
Peer's Cave

Abseiling
Table Mountain

Air

Paragliding/Hang-gliding
Silvermine (designated site)
Lion's Head (designated site)
Table Mountain
Devil's Peak
Signal Hill
Little Lion's Head/Llandudno
Noordhoek Peak

sequinned apron. A traditional braai and animated storytelling with songs sung in resonant harmony by the Xhosa guides soon have trailists blissfully happy in African la-la-land. The trail ends the following day at the foot of Nursery Ravine in Kirstenbosch Gardens, the first botanical garden in the world to be named a UNESCO World Heritage Site.

The two-day People's Trail (14.9km/15½ miles) is an educational trail aimed at youth groups. Beginning at Constantia Nek, it tracks Disa gorge through indigenous afromontane forest, emerging in *fynbos* on the mountain back-table. Time is spent at the Waterworks Museum, with an overnight stay in a dormitory-style hut. The trail ends with a descent of Platteklip gorge to the lower cableway station.

The most awaited trails, though, are the Tip to Top and Top to Tip pair, still in the process of being established. These guided six-day hikes will have trailists carrying their own rucksacks, food and sleeping bags, and overnighting in platformed tents built of recycled alien trees. The route starts at Cape Point, tracing the sandstone and granite backbone of the Peninsula mountain massif all the way to the front face of Table Mountain – or vice versa. Included in this bracing encounter with nature's finery are stupendous views from clifftops plunging dramatically into the thrashing ocean, air-brushed

National park must-do's

mountainscapes on distant horizons, Noordhoek's lonely curve of whiter-than-white beach, the smouldering (in season) ember-red to sulphur-yellow *fynbos* scrub, and giant fractured boulders reminding you of the relentless powers of fire, water and ice.

The first phase of the Tip to Top trail opened in August 2006, encompassing a guided, portered and catered two-day walk from Silvermine dam to a tented camp in Orange Kloof, set in afromontane forest of, among others, False Ironwood (*Olea capensis*), Real Yellowwood (*Podocarpus latifolius*) and Cape Beech (*Rapanea melanophloeos*). A walk via Disa gorge to the cableway station ends with a swift zip down the mountain by cable car.

National park must-do's
360° views by cable car
Visitors who like the fit and active approach to life have over 350 routes by which to summit Table Mountain but remember, they range from easy to very difficult. Any route, whether simple or tricky, should be planned in utmost detail as the weather is highly capricious on these mountain slopes and paths can be narrow, steep and slippery. The most skilled mountaineers have lost their footing (and their lives) on these well-worn tracks. Otherwise, in the time it takes the rotating floor of the cableway's hi-tech bubble car to turn full circle, you can be whisked some 1000m (3281ft) high in way under 10 minutes. The wraparound views at the top will leave you speechless.

Chapman's Peak to Cape Point
This famous coastal road is cut so sharply into the mountainside, nets have had to be built to catch periodical tumbling boulders; there's not much between you and the cobalt sea lying a sheer cliff-drop below you. Marvel at the scythe-like swathe cut by Noordhoek's pristine sands, then try to catch a glimpse of a curly-horned, white-nosed bontebok in the Cape of Good Hope reserve. At Cape Point, the Flying Dutchman funicular eases your journey to a lookout above wild untamed seas. Be very wary of the chacma baboons, who've become particularly bold and brazen in their search for food; at no cost should you feed them. On the return journey around the Peninsula's tip, Simon's Town, Fish Hoek and Kalk Bay each display their own scenic or historical charm.

Trail Rehabilitation

• Almost 450 individuals from disadvantaged communities have been enlisted to forge the paths making up the Hoerikwaggo trails.

• Path-making has entailed hauling and removing rocks, repairing gabions (wire/steel nets supporting rock fortification) and building signage.

• 450 tons of rock have been moved to create a 700km (435-mile) intricate maze of paths.

• Xhosa-speaking guides from disadvantaged backgrounds have undergone rigorous training in the ways of the mountain and are also rehearsed in the ancient art of storytelling.

Reptiles

Boomslang
Puff adder
Southern rock agama (blue head)
Black girdled lizard (prehistoric looks)
Cape skink (suns on rocks)

Table Mountain National Park

Boulders' penguin colony

From two breeding pairs in the early 1980s, this protected colony of African (jackass) penguins, which has selected the prettiest of beaches as their nesting abode, has expanded to several thousand individuals. Having colonized Boulders Beach, they've given rise to a major tourist site where an extensive elevated boardwalk allows visitors to get up close and personal (well, almost) with these comical waddling birds, whose appetite for pilchards and anchovies has them busting out of their tuxedos. Depending on the season, you will have black-and-white faces peering quizzically at you from every rock and sand crevice. Chicks are prolific between March and September.

When to visit

Winters are generally cold, stormy and wet (May–July); spring brings out all the wild flowers, but can still be chilly at times (snow often sprinkles mountain peaks into October); summers are cloudless and hot, often accompanied by the wild Southeaster. The warm, mild autumn months (Feb–Mar) are glorious.

Accommodation

Olifantsbos
Whitewashed, pitch-roofed Cape-style cottage plonked amongst *fynbos* right at the sea's edge in the southern part of Cape of Good Hope reserve; 3 bedrooms (linen provided), fully equipped kitchen, fireplace, patio/braai; solar power. Tel: +27-(0)21-7809204 (Buffelsfontein visitor centre).

Eland and Duiker cottages
Stone and wood-panelled cottages with large wooden-framed windows in Cape of Good Hope reserve; each has 3 bedrooms (linen provided), fully equipped kitchen, fireplace. Duiker cottage has *boma*/braai. Tel: +27-(0)21-7809204 (Buffelsfontein).

Wood Owl cottage
Characterful restored forester's cottage in Tokai pine plantation on slopes of Constantiaberg, fully equipped; thatch roof, high ceilings, wooden floors; 3 bedrooms en suite, fireplace; patio/braai area. Tel: +27-(0)21-7127471 (Tokai office).

For images of the accommodation: visit the park's official website (*see* Contact details, page 123).

Contact details

Left: The sheer number and variety of plant species in their natural environment, nestled at the foot of the Peninsula mountain chain, makes Kirstenbosch one of Cape Town's top five visitor attractions.

Contact details
Table Mountain National Park official website:
www.sanparks.org/parks/table_mountain
General enquiries: tel: +27-(0)21-7018692
e-mail: tablemountain@sanparks.org

For all info on adventure activities:
Cape Town Tourism, tel: +27-(0)21-4876800
e-mail: capetown@tourismcapetown.co.za
website: www.tourismcapetown.co.za

Permits for hang-gliding/paragliding: tel: +27-(0)21-7018692

Hiking/Climbing: Mountain Club of South Africa,
tel: +27-(0)21-4653412, e-mail: mcsacapetown@iafrica.com
Cape Town School of Mountaineering, tel: +27-(0)21-5314290
e-mail: climb@ctsm.co.za

Hoerikwaggo hiking trails: tel: +27-(0)21-4658515
e-mail: hoerikwaggobookings@sanparks.co.za
website: www.hoerikwaggotrails.co.za

Table Mountain aerial cableway:
Hours: 08:30 to 07:00–10:00 (depending on season);
website: www.tablemountain.org

An Adrenaline Fix by Sea

Scuba diving
Atlantic coast 11–15°C (52–59°F)
False Bay 14–19°C (57–66°F)
Clifton–Camps Bay
Oudekraal
Karbonkelberg/Hout Bay
Glencairn
Seaforth–Miller's Point
Miller's Point–Smitswinkel Bay

Shark cage-diving
(Great white sharks)
Seal Island/False Bay
Dyer Island/Gansbaai
Mossel Bay

Dolphins and Whales
(Common, bottlenose and dusky dolphin; humpback and southern right whale)
Offshore Cape Peninsula

ADDO ELEPHANT NATIONAL PARK AND SHAMWARI GAME RESERVE

The oldest, and smallest, sector of Addo Elephant National Park – today making up only one-tenth of the entire reserve – was established in 1931 to promote the survival of only 11 African elephant which, from 1900 onwards, had evaded the guns of 19th- and early 20th-century hunters and merciless neighbouring farmers. In response to the persistent lobbying by farm-owners, the government had actually commissioned one dubious Major Philip Pretorius to eradicate the free-roaming gentle giants – which he almost did, bringing down 114 elephant between 1919 and 1920. Only in 1954 did the park manager at the time, Graham Armstrong, succeed in conclusively safeguarding these threatened mammals when he devised an elephant-proof fence of tram rails and elevator cables, mapping out a 23km² (9-sq-mile) protected area; the elephant count stood at 22 individuals. This fencing construction, now dubbed 'Armstrong fence', is still used by the park today.

The gene pool of Addo's elephants differs from any other in the country; this is believed to be the result of selective shooting during the 19th-century hunting excursions. The tusks brandished by the elephant population's bulls are small, while most cows don't display tusks at all.

Park Statistics

Location: 72km (45 miles) north of Port Elizabeth.
Size: Over 1480km² (570 sq miles) plus 1200km² (464 sq miles) marine protected area.
5-star factor: Over 450 elephant.
Of interest: A diversity of habitats (5 biomes) and changing landscapes.

Opposite, top to bottom:
Addo's focus is the protection of elephants, which it has done with great success; the accommodation in the Shamwari Game Reserve is superb and architecturally diverse; the Zuurberg mountains in Addo are wild trail territory.

Addo Elephant National Park

The Modern Scarab

To the observant visitor, large, often horned, dung beetles are a conspicuous sight in wildlife reserves. They belong to the large family Scarabaeidae – which hints at the fact that these particular insects were the ones viewed in ancient Egyptian times as sacred symbols (scarabs). These very industrious creatures will be seen tenaciously rolling their balls of dung, with their hind legs, either to a suitable nearby spot for sustenance or to bury it in a hole – which is the male beetle's duty. Here the female lays a single egg so that when it hatches, the larva can feed on the dung. The beetles locate elephant, rhino and buffalo dung by positioning themselves downwind, then flying backwards and forwards across the wind to pick up any scent, which they can identify from a considerable distance. They are capable of scattering a dropping in an impressively short space of time.

SANParks has plans for Addo to become, eventually, a megapark of 3600km² (1390 sq miles); this will include the recently added (2005) marine protected area encompassing the rippled barrier of the Alexandria dunes – largest coastal dunefield in the southern hemisphere – and Bird and Seal islands (St Croix is a proposed future addition). Addo will in turn become South Africa's fourth largest national park (after Kruger, Kgalagadi and St Lucia).

The Addo Elephant National Park is in fact a disparate collection of pockets of land loosely cobbled together. Starting in the south are the offshore islands; then, along the shoreline, Woody Cape which spans the coast between two river mouths – Bushman's River to the east, Sundays River to the west – and the Alexandria dunefield; and next, two Colchester sections. From here the reserve spans the original park territory, before curving in a boomerang shape to the Nyathi, Zuurberg mountain and Kabouga sections, ending in the northwest with the Darlington dam area.

Biomes by the handful

Addo is justly proud of its five out of seven (generally accepted) biomes in South Africa. For the most part, the park features Subtropical Thicket, or valley bushveld, a biome that takes up 69% of the reserve – that is, in the original Addo section and the

Right: The Aloe claviflora begins with a single plant that continuously divides to become a profusion of fleshy leaves that form a circle. This gives rise to its common name, the kraal aloe, alluding to the circular hut settlements of South Africa's indigenous people.

Biomes by the handful

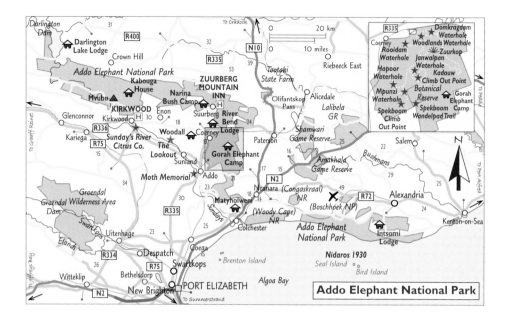

Colchester, Nyathi and Kabouga areas. It is dense, sometimes impenetrable low forest consisting of shrubs, vines, and evergreen or succulent trees – tall spiky aloes and euphorbias – and, in particular, the Spekboom. Known in English as Porkbush (*Portulacaria afra*), its trunk is a shiny red-brown to grey, and in October/November the densely leaved tree is covered in a profusion of pink flower sprays. African women reportedly chew the leaves if they're struggling to produce milk for their babies. Look also for the Karoo Boer-bean (*Schotia afra*) with its fine feathery leaves – rows of tiny leaflets along a central stalk – and woody oblong flattened seed pods. In spring, the trees' scarlet blooms splash the dry bushveld with fiery verve.

The Forest biome occurs along parts of Alexandria's dunescape where the giant slopes are thickly wooded, while beneath the rippling desert sands lining the shore lie valuable cultural repositories of archaeological interest – ancient middens that once belonged to the nomadic Strandlopers. Shells, animal bones, fragments of pottery and stone implements all provide evidence of a people that has since disappeared from these shores.

Addo Elephant National Park

Animal Life

The main players
African elephant
Buffalo
Black rhino
Hippopotamus (Sundays River)
Predators
Lion
Leopard
Spotted hyena
Black-backed jackal
VIP antelope
Gemsbok
Red hartebeest
Eland
Red List
Oribi (reintroduced July 2006)

Bird Life

Addo Rest Camp
Bokmakierie
Southern Tchagra
Brown-hooded Kingfisher
Fiscal Flycatcher
Fork-tailed Drongo
Alexandria forest
Cape Parrot
Knysna Turaco (Lourie)
Grey Cuckoo-shrike
Bird Island
Cape Gannet
African (Jackass) Penguin
Roseate Tern

The Zuurberg zone, straddling the folded sedimentary mountain foothills, falls under both Grassland and *Fynbos* biomes and Addo's furthest extremity, around Darlington dam, displays Nama Karoo biome characteristics. Be on the lookout here for the smaller details – the fleshy pebble-like Stone Plant (*Lithops ruschiorum*), the dainty blue Karoo Daisy (*Felicia australis*) – and, back at eye-level again, tiny yellow-button acacias like sweet thorn.

From tree dassie to black rhino

This variance in vegetation also determines the type of animal that calls Addo home so, for example, bushpig, tree dassie and the brown hyena – which are generally restricted to arid, desert-like areas and sandy coastal strips – hide out in Alexandria's coastal dune forest. Here the hyena scavenge for food, supplementing with insects and fruit. Meanwhile, Zuurberg's mountain territory is the domain of dainty blue duiker and mountain reedbuck, sure-footed Cape mountain zebra, and aardwolf, distinguished by the vertical stripes on its flanks. This hyena-like animal roams the park at night, snuffling out termites. Gemsbok thrive in Darlington's dry Karoo zone, but this is also the home range of the heavyweights – black rhino, buffalo and black wildebeest. Addo's plan is to introduce cheetah and wild dog here once the park expansion is complete. Of interest is that Addo's limited grassveld has influenced its buffalo population into modifying their eating habits; normally grazers in high-rainfall zones, these buffalo were driven by hunters to seek refuge in Addo's bushveld, where they adapted to browsing among the trees mainly in the coolness of night. As a result, they generally have not been that visible during the day. Recently, though, the reintroduction of lion has forced them to change their habits once again – they now prefer the safety of daylight versus the anonymity their predators gain under the cloak of darkness.

Of the reserve's black rhino population, two different subspecies exist. The first, *Diceros bicornis bicornis*, naturally occurs in Southern Africa's reserves, while the other, *Diceros bicornis michaeli*, was introduced to Addo from East Africa. Both share similar features, most notably the pointed upper lip, or hook-lip, of the black rhinoceros versus the wide, square muzzle of white rhinos. The two species are kept in different sections of the reserve so as not to mix the gene pool.

Hiking

Finally, the incorporation of the marine park has added another feather to Addo's cap in the form of the world's largest Cape Gannet breeding colony on Bird Island (reportedly some 120 000 birds), as well as Roseate Terns, and the second-largest breeding colony of African (Jackass) Penguins.

Hiking

A range of hiking trails (1–4 hours) penetrates the Zuurberg's deep forested kloofs, promising exciting chittering bird life, and along the coastline, the two-day Alexandria hiking trail crests sharply defined slip faces of the undulating dunefields stretching for 50km (30 miles) northward of Algoa Bay. Here too are fossil dune ridges marking previous shorelines going back a few million years. Look out for whales and dolphins from the high tops of the dune cliffs. This 36km (22-mile) trail traverses the forested Woody Cape sector, with an overnight stay in a scenically sited wood hut, before setting out for the coastal dunefields.

When to visit

January daily max 32°C (90°F); July 18°C (64°F), although each park sector will experience climatic variations specific to habitat. Rainfall low but peaks Feb–Mar and Oct–Nov. Park entrance gate open from 07:00 to 19:00.

Nature on Wheels and Foot

The wilder, more untamed areas of the Addo Elephant Park lend themselves to (not so intrepid) exploration – and the choice is horseback, 4x4 or your own trusty two feet. Guided horse trails for novices through experienced riders vary from one to five hours, weaving their unobtrusive way through the older elephant preserve or striking out into the dramatic Zuurberg mountain landscapes. This scoured, buckled territory and the Kabouga section are also where six hours of 4x4 trails trace the hardy routes forged by the wagon wheels of the early pioneers, fording rivers while ancient cycads stand sentinel on rugged steep slopes. Hippo cavort in the Sunday River and wildlife lurks in the tangled valley bushveld, so keep your vision skills honed.

Left: Hunting, predators and sparse vegetation have forced Addo's buffalo population to change its grazing habits over the years.

Addo Elephant National Park

Accommodation

The **main rest camp** is located near Addo town; it has a restaurant, a shop and a pool. Accommodation (all with equipped kitchens) consists of the following:

Guesthouses: Two houses, Hapoor and Domkrag, for up to 6 persons, on floodlit water hole; air-conditioned.

Below: The developing embryo of a baby elephant spends 22 months in its mother's womb. Young elephant are born at any time of the year and may live for 60 to 70 years. Elephant in general display a high level of intelligence, they have sophisticated methods of communication and a complex social structure. When herds gather together at a watering hole, visitors will observe them greeting each other with affection.

Chalets: Whitewashed, A-frame thatched buildings, from 3-person bedsitter to 6 persons; air-conditioned. Two chalets adapted for physically impaired.

Cottages: 2 persons, kitchenette, ceiling fan.

Rondavels: Stone-and-thatch buildings on floodlit water hole; air-conditioned; communal kitchen.

Forest cabins: wooden, A-frame structures for 4 persons; single room with beds, table and chairs, fridge; bathroom; communal kitchen, braai facilities.

Safari tents: on wooden deck raised on stilts, located in the camping area; for 2 persons; fan, fridge; communal kitchen and ablution facilities.

Caravan and camp sites: communal kitchen and ablution facilities.

Main Addo Section
Gorah Elephant Camp: privately run luxury tented camp; tel: +27-(0)44-5327818, website: www.gorah.com

Colchester Section
Camp Matyholweni: in south of park; white-walled, wooden-beamed, thatched self-catering chalets with clay floor tiles; for 2–4 persons; tel: +27-(0)41-4680916, e-mail: Matyholweni@sanparks.org

Nyathi Concession
River Bend Lodge: luxury, 5-star, eight rooms; wellness centre; tel: +27-(0)42-2338000, website: www.riverbend.za.com

Addo Accommodation

Zuurberg Section

Narina Bush Camp: tented camp with 4 x 2-person tents next to Witrivier in Zuurberg mountains; no electricity; equipped kitchen; flush toilet, paraffin-heated shower. *Lapa*/braai area. Accessible by car but can also be reached on horseback. All bookings Addo park reception.

Darlington Dam Section

Darlington Lake Lodge: 5 luxury rooms, 7 furnished tents; tel: +27-(0)42-2433673, e-mail darlington@eastcape.net

Alexandria Dunefields

Intsomi Lodge: near town of Alexandria; 8 luxury chalets; wellness centre; tel: +27-(0)46-6538903/4/5, e-mail: Intsomi@telkomsa.net website: www.intsomi.co.za

Contact details

Addo Elephant National Park reception,
tel. no. +27-(0)42-2330556/7, e-mail: reservations@sanparks.org
website: www.addoelephantpark.com

Above: Gorah Elephant Camp, a private concession in Addo, consists of a colonial manor house dating to 1856 (and today a national monument) and 11 luxurious tented suites sheltered under thatched canopies. The camp's ambience recreates the elegance of African safaris of the early 1900s. Guests are able to settle in on the manor's verandah and watch a daily parade of wildlife slaking their thirst at a perfectly placed water hole.

Shamwari Game Reserve

Shamwari Game Reserve

Its southern border cupped by the Bushmans River, this private game reserve prides itself on its rich contingent of wildlife whose daily movements are tracked and monitored by a phalanx of trained and highly skilled guides. Guests at the reserve's impressive collection of lodges, each with its own character, are plied with care and personal attention as they're ushered into open Land Rovers for long dawn and dusk drives, leaving the middle of the day for swimming, relaxation and utter tranquillity. This pampering and focusing on the finer details has garnered Shamwari a fistful of international awards, among them World's Leading Conservation Company and Private Game Reserve for five consecutive years. Not much to find fault with here ...

Those who prefer to get within pumping heartbeat range of Africa's wildest creatures can embark on a bush walk, chaperoned by armed rangers who also educate them on the subtler aspects of the veld – spoor markings, characteristics of animal behaviour, disturbed plants and trees indicating the passing of an animal – the things generally missed in a vehicle. The rangers are also excellent at spotting birds and identifying their calls and flight patterns.

Visitors who need to rest their eyes from peering into impenetrable vegetation and deciphering the difference between animal camouflage and the bush palette's play on shadow and light can take a trip to the nearby African arts and culture village, Khaya Lendaba. Here, insight is gained into cultural traditions, indigenous healing methods, dance and traditional dishes of the Eastern Cape's Xhosa people and other tribal groups.

Sleeptime ... and spoilt for choice

Because accommodation in Shamwari (the word means 'friend') focuses on contrasts in architectural flavour and ambience, it's worth dwelling on some of these different characteristics. Graceful **Long Lee Manor**, a restored Edwardian mansion built in 1910 by the descendants of an early settler from York, England, looks onto the plains fronting the Bushmans River; open-air meals can be relished here at the river *lapa*. **Eagles Crag Lodge**, venturing into avant-garde design, features

Park Statistics

Location: north of Port Elizabeth, 65km (40 miles) along N2 to Grahamstown, 7km (4 miles) on the R342.
Size: 200km² (77 sq miles).
5-star factor: Big cat sightings.
Of interest: 6 luxury bush lodges, each with own architectural character and ambience.

Animal Life

Big Five
Lion
Leopard
Elephant
Black (and White) rhino
Buffalo
Rarer seen mammals
Wild dog
Brown hyena
Aardwolf
Serval
Caracal

Shamwari Accommodation

separate glass-walled units of thatch and stone tucked into the valley under the protective canopy of tall trees; all have a private deck and plunge pool with uninterrupted vistas of the bushveld. A Wellness Spa is the cherry on the top for personal time out.

Bushmans Lodge is a restored Victorian homestead, replete with high ceilings, wooden floors and checkered bathroom tiles in black and white. A thatched *boma* stands above the wooded valley, where the Bushmans River snakes through thick vegetation.

Just five luxury rooms form part of **Lobengula Lodge** with its wooden-beamed, thatched architecture and dark-wood ethnic décor, while the larger **Riverdene Lodge** offers guests two elegant casual lounges, a sunroom and a jewel-blue rim-flow pool. The tented luxury of **Bayethe Lodge** seems hard to beat. Meaning 'I salute you', Bayethe's thatched and tent-walled en-suite units each have a pool on a private deck suspended above the river; they are also heated or air conditioned, depending on ambient temperature. The deck is the perfect perch from which to glimpse a Crowned Eagle's wing span up above or an antelope slaking its thirst down below.

When to Visit

Summer Nov–Jan; winter May–Jul (see Addo for temperatures). Game-viewing conditions are excellent year-round.

For information and accommodation, tel: +27-(0)42-2031111

e-mail: reservations@shamwari.com

website: www.shamwari.com

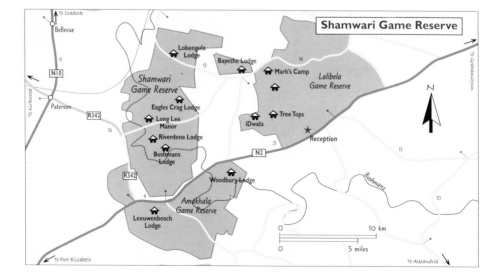

KAROO NATIONAL PARK AND MOUNTAIN ZEBRA NATIONAL PARK

In an effort to preserve the unique Karoo-type habitat that surrounds Beaufort West, 72km² (28 sq miles) of land was donated to SANParks by Beaufort's town council in 1979 to create the nucleus of today's national park. Subsequently expanded to its present size, the park is characterized by stark, denuded landscapes kneaded to the furthest horizon, punctuated only by sharp-edged dolerite koppies rearing up from the flat plains. What imprints itself on your consciousness is the sense of miles and miles of unfettered space. No imprint made by civilization, no city lights, no communication towers – simply the purity of silence.

Vegetation is sparse on these sculpted plains, softened only by montane Karoo shrub and Karoo succulent and grassy dwarf-shrub-type vegetation. Here, the desiccated environs give rise to plant names like biltongbos, and thorny bushes whose sharp hooks (*doring*) form the basis of descriptive Afrikaans labels – wolwedoring and drie- and kriedoring.

Park Statistics

Location: 450km (280 miles) from Cape Town; about 1000km (620 miles) south of Johannesburg; entry gate 2.5km (1.5 miles) south of Beaufort West.
Size: 800km² (295 sq miles).
5-star factor: Pure air and infinite space extending to every horizon.
Of interest: Quagga breeding programme.

Opposite, top to bottom: The Karoo, sometimes dominated by buckled mountains like the Nuweveldberge, generally is about infinite space and dry, dusty horizons; mountain zebra (centre) are suitably sure-footed for their high terrain.

Karoo National Park

Animal Life

Black rhino released (2005) into 80km² (29-sq-mile) camp
Cape mountain zebra
Burchell's zebra
Horned and hoofed
Black wildebeest
Red hartebeest
Eland
Kudu
Springbok
Reptilian
5 Tortoise spp.
Terrapin sp.
Spiny agama
Monitor spp.

Horizonless vistas

The difficult terrain precludes a developed road network, but there are two routes negotiable in a normal sedan vehicle. The 13km (8-mile) Lammertjiesleegte circular route across the plains usually complies with eager visitors' expectations by yielding excellent game-viewing, while the bracing route up to the Klipspringer Pass (12km/7 miles from the entrance gate) rises from the flatlands to an intermediate plateau via Andrew Geddes Bain's impressively constructed pass of dry-wall cliffs. Beyond this is 4x4 territory, however.

Another worthwhile sedan-car drive is that to the Mountain View self-catering huts which line the scarp of the Nuweveld mountain plateau. Sweeping views unfold across the town of Beaufort West and surrounding Karoo landscape. The drive there first exits the park, then re-enters 3km (2 miles) north of Beaufort West, climbs Molteno Pass and meanders for some time before backtracking to the mountain edge.

A series of rugged 4x4 trails can be undertaken, accompanied by a guide or independently in your own vehicle. They head across roller-flat plains, around eroded rock and up to the intermediate plateau, hugging precarious cliff edges and summiting rocky mountain passes. A parks brochure details nuggets of interest to note along the way. A century-old restored shepherd's cottage affords tired but inspired travellers a comfortable roof for the night.

Right: The Fossil Trail reveals calcified bone fragments of ancient giant creatures dating back 255 million years.

255-million-year-old fossils

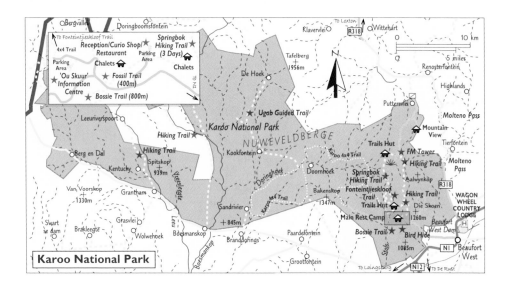

Karoo National Park

255-million-year-old fossils

The national park rest camp, a collection of thatched A-frame Cape vernacular cottages settled on the plains, is embraced by the surrounding mountainscapes. It's the launch point for three short walking trails, the first (the Fossil Trail) only 400m (437yd); this is described in greater detail below. The second, the Bossie Trail, over 800m (875yd), identifies 65 specific Karoo-type plants via labels and an accompanying brochure. The 10km (6-mile) Pointer's Hiking Trail invites walkers to revel in the Karoo air and the solitude under great open skies.

Most fascinating of all is the shortest walk, the Fossil Trail. The Karoo is a highly valuable repository for fossils that can be dated to between 300 and 150 million years ago. Southern Africa, approximately 300 million years ago, was still part of the supercontinent Gondwana and along its southern extremity formed a massive mountain belt. At the time, the Karoo was in fact a vast sea. Rivers from the mountain massif carried sediments to the sea, and it is this layer of sedimentation that managed to preserve the remains of animal life, which either became trapped in the mud or perished as warmer climates caused the ocean to recede.

Bird Life

Raptors
Verreaux's (Black) Eagle
Booted Eagle
African Harrier Hawk (Gymnogene)
Steppe Buzzard
Rock Kestrel

Karoo specials
Yellow-bellied Eremomola
Karoo Eremomola
Karoo Korhaan
Namaqua Warbler
Karoo Scrub Robin

Intriguing monikers
Chestnut-vented Tit-babbler
Cinnamon-breasted Bunting
Pririt Batis

Karoo National Park

Is the Quagga a Zebra?

Since the 1970s, Reinhold Rau, a South African taxidermist working at the Natural History Museum, Cape Town, has made it his life's work to breed the once-extinct quagga into renewed existence. This horse-like mammal died out in 1883 as a result of indiscriminate shooting by 18th-century British hunters and overzealous 19th-century farmers. Rau firmly believes the quagga is a subspecies of plains, or Burchell's, zebra. It was distinguished by a brown colouring to its hide and a complete lack of stripes across the back torso area, rump and legs; brown and white stripes appeared only across the face, neck, shoulders and front flanks. In 1986, using a group of plains zebra (donated by the Namibian National Parks Board) with stripe markings most closely resembling those of a quagga, Rau has been mating them from one generation to the next, breeding out the uncharacteristic stripes. In 1998, 14 of the Quagga Project zebras were translocated into the Karoo National Park. Rau's greatest success, in 2005, was a third-generation foal descended from the original zebra group. It features some of the quagga's brown colouring and an absence of stripes on the rump; solely the stripes across the middle joint of its hind legs give the game away of this would-be 'quagga'.

The Fossil Trail, upgraded in 2005, is a stone-paved walkway lined with glass display cases containing the intriguing fossils and casts of mammal-like reptiles belonging to the Therapsid group. Fully intact skeletons, skulls and bones are sometimes 255 million years old, existing at a time known as the Permian period. A couple of the most memorable include the gruesome sharp-honed teeth of the sleek, fleet-footed, wolf-like carnivore, Gorgonopsian, and a skeleton belonging to the herbivore, Bradysaurus.

The displays are numbered and tie up with a detailed brochure, while a guide rope and Braille plates encourage the visually impaired to share in the Karoo's ancient secrets.

For rugged outdoor-loving nature enthusiasts, the three-day Springbok Hiking Trail covers 26.5km (16½ miles) of Karoo territory, from bossie-dotted plain to a king-of-the-castle perch at the top of the giant-bouldered Nuweberg.

When to visit

Summers are very hot, but subzero temperatures occur in winter with snow on Nuweveld mountain peaks; Mar–Oct are the best months to visit.

Accommodation

Main Rest Camp

Restaurant, shop, information centre, pool. Thatched, whitewashed, A-frame Cape vernacular-style cottages, 2 bedrooms en suite, fully equipped kitchen. Also 1-bedroom self-catering cottages, lounge/kitchenette, bathroom. Cape vernacular-style chalets, bathroom, basically equipped kitchenette; facilities for physically impaired. Camp/caravan sites.

Mountain View Rest Camp

Mountain retreat with huts, up to 25 persons, basic facilities, communal ablution block.

Contact details

For information and reservations, tel: +27-(0)23-4152828/9
e-mail: reservations@sanparks.org
website: www.sanparks.org/parks/karoo

Mountain Zebra National Park

This park's small size belies its beautiful setting and abundance of large antelope and shyer, daintier buck. Star of its wildlife stage is, of course, the Cape mountain zebra whose survival in the 1930s was highly tenuous. In 1937, there were only six animals of this zebra species on the farm Babylon's Toren, which in that same year was proclaimed a national park in an effort to protect them. By 1949 only two Cape mountain zebra had survived. Rescue came in the form of 11 zebra that a local farmer generously offered to the national park, and in 1964 a count of 25 Cape mountain zebra was recorded in the park logbook. The Mountain Zebra National Park has since increased in size, additional zebra have been introduced, and from here they are reintroduced into other protected areas.

Park Statistics

Location: 24km (15 miles) from Cradock; 280km (174 miles) from Port Elizabeth.
Size: 65km² (25 sq miles).
5-star factor: Cape mountain zebra conservation success story.
Of interest: Sweeping views and grazing wildlife on Rooiplaat's heights.

Sweet-grass plains and rocky ridges

The most striking physical feature of the park is the densely wooded tract of the Wilgeboom River as it cuts a well-watered path diagonally across the entire preserve. Its thickly shaded banks carry Karee (*Rhus lancea*), Sweet Thorn (*Acacia karroo*), Wild Olive (*Olea europaea*), and White Stinkwood (*Celtis africana*) – which, incidentally, has absolutely no relation to the true stinkwood. In contrast are the great open grassveld plains unravelling into the distance under puff-cloud skies until they encounter the circular dolerite-capped hills of the Bankberg to the southeast. From here an imposing ridge fuses into the Rooiplaat plateau, where the park veers off at a tangent to the northwest. The plateau's juicy grassveld lures much of the grazing wildlife to its upland reaches, so game-viewing is at a

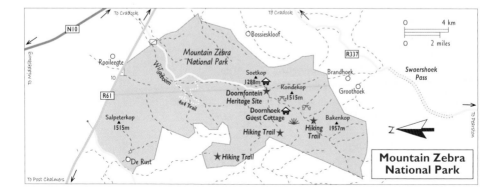

Mountain Zebra
National Park

Mountain Zebra National Park

Contact Details

Visit www.parks-sa.co.za or www.
sanparks.org/parks/mountain_zebra
For information and reservations:
park tel: +27 (O)48-8812427/3434.
SANParks reservations:
tel: +27 (O)12-3431991 or
e-mail: reservations@parks-sa.co.za

Blueprint – Cape Mountain Zebra

Easiest characteristic to spot in the Cape mountain zebra is that its hide doesn't feature the grey shadow-stripes of the Burchell's (plains) species. Its black stripes are also narrower than the Burchell's and they stop short of the belly, leaving it white. You can also spot a Cape mountain zebra by the orange-brown coloration on its muzzle and face. Throughout the different species, each zebra's stripes (like fingerprints) never match up to any other individual's stripe pattern and even differ to either side of the body. Cape mountain zebra prefer the higher grasslands of the plateaus and in winter they are proactive in moving up to mountain slopes and ravines to find grazing.

premium here. The rocky round hills are prettified in winter with flowering salmon-pink Coral Aloe (*Aloe striata*) and the distinctive Mountain Cabbage, or Kiepersol (*Cussonia paniculata*), with its umbrella-like leaves and candelabra spray of flowers thrusting through the leafy canopy.

Vegetation unique to this Karoo landscape includes a plethora of hardy bushes, among them the fragant Wild Camphor Bush (*Tarchonanthus camphoratus*), and a couple that have been so colourfully labelled in the local lingo they defy translation: Koggelmandervoetkaroo and Witmuistepelkaroo. You'll get a better analysis from a park guide.

On wheels and on foot

Visitors will get a good taste of the park's scenic and animal-life attributes by setting out on the 24km (15-mile) circular driving route from the Mountain Zebra National Park rest camp. It meanders up to the elevated heights of Rooiplaat, with its panoramas over expansive plains interrupted by low rounded bushes, then descends to the southwestern border before doubling back, all the while hugging the verdant river valley. Off the Rooiplaat road is a San rock art site featuring human figures, antelope and other smaller animals in black and ochre colour stains; it can be visited with a park guide.

For a more intimate experience of the wilds, a number of walks range from the hour-long Bossieskloof, with its viewpoint over the park and across to the granite ridge-tops of the Bankberg, to the three-day Mountain Zebra Hiking Trail. Overnighting in natural-material stone huts with basic amenities (hot showers included), the trail threads through the park's most appealing features – traversing wooded kloofs, crossing rocky ridges, circumnavigating perfectly round hills, and encountering the many streams that feed the Wilgeboom River (*wilger* is Afrikaans for 'willow', *boom* denotes 'tree'). Day two of the trail climbs Bakenkop (some 2000m/6560ft), in the reserve's southeastern extreme. Trailists will no doubt interrupt Cape mountain zebra and various antelope nibbling on leaves and sweet grasses.

A third 10km (6-mile) day walk crosses a portion of the three-day trail, up and down shady kloofs and passing the only sandstone

Accommodation

hill in the park, Rondekop. A gigantic 6000-tonne boulder, which ripped away from this rock outcrop 30 years ago and gouged a path down the hillslope, is visible from the trail path.

In holiday season, visitors can request horse-riding excursions, a unique way to interact with the park's wildlife.

Where accommodation is concerned, of particular interest is Doornhoek Guest Cottage. Dating to 1836, this restored Victorian home's claim to fame is the role it played as the setting for the movie *Story of an African Farm*, based on Olive Schreiner's famous South African novel. Schreiner, who gained recognition as a fierce campaigner for human rights and equality among women, worked as a governess in the Cradock area in the 1830s. Her novel was first published in 1883 under the pseudonym Ralph Iron; she died in 1920.

Since Doornhoek so perfectly embodied the typical Eastern Cape farmhouse of the 1930s, it was chosen as the focal point of the film, which also stars South African export Richard E Grant, born in Swaziland but riding a successful film career today in the UK.

When to visit
Summer is very hot (Nov–Jan) so it is best to avoid the area at this time. Peaks are regularly snow-frosted in winter, but the days are warm; rainfall occurs Jan–Apr.

Accommodation
Main Rest Camp
Luxury 4-bed stone cottages, partially equipped kitchen; caravan/ camp sites; restaurant, shop, fuel, pool at base of granite ridge.

Doornhoek Guest Cottage (National Monument)
Self-catering for 6 persons; traditional furnishings, copper door handles, stained-glass windows, yellowwood ceilings, Oregon pine floors.

Mountain trail stone huts
Bunks/mattresses, shower/toilet, basic cooking utensils.

Animal Life

Cape mountain zebra
Black-backed jackal
Newly introduced
Black rhino
Buffalo
Horned and hoofed
Black wildebeest
Red hartebeest
Eland, Kudu, Springbok
Small antelope spp.
Feline creatures
Caracal
African wild cat
Black-footed (Small spotted) cat

Bird Life

Terrestrial
Ostrich
Secretary Bird
Blue Crane
Denham's (Stanley's) Bustard
Raptors
Jackal Buzzard
Verreaux's (Black) Eagle
Booted Eagle
Martial Eagle
Specials
Fairy Flycatcher
Eastern Clapper
Thick-billed Lark
Melodious Lark
Sickle-winged Chat
Namaqua Warbler

NATIONAL PARKS GUIDE

Other South African National Parks

Western Cape
West Coast National Park

Just inland from the harbour of Saldanha Bay is Langebaan Lagoon, focal point of this 276km^2 (106-sq-mile) park. Tens of thousands of migratory palaearctic waders flock to the lagoon, and the offshore islands of Schaapen, Jutten, Marcus and Malgas support breeding colonies of African (Jackass) Penguins, Cape Gannets and cormorants. In season, pelicans, flamingos and African Black Oystercatchers congregate on Langebaan's shores. The Postberg Flower Reserve opens in spring, where eland, red hartebeest, wildebeest and others graze in kaleidoscopic-hued grasslands.

Bontebok National Park

Cradled to one side by the imposing Langeberg mountain range and the broad band of the Breede River to the other, this 300km^2 (116-sq-mile) park near Swellendam was established to save the last few remaining bontebok from extinction; numbers have risen from a seriously endangered 17 in around 1931 to way beyond 200 today. The *fynbos* vegetation supports many antelope species, including red hartebeest. Bird life is excellent (just under 200 species).

Wilderness National Park

A 30km (20-mile) coastal stretch from the Touw River mouth to the Swartvlei estuary and beyond, and linking with the Goukamma Nature Reserve, expands landward to embrace five lakes – Eilandvlei, Langvlei, Rondevlei, Swartvlei and Groenvlei. A freshwater channel, the Serpentine, winds its way from the Touw River, where the picturesque Ebb-and-Flow wood-cabin rest camp lies, to Eilandvlei. At this Ramsar site, naturalists can enjoy wave-washed beaches, mountains, and both fresh- and saltwater lakes and estuaries. Water-bird species are prolific.

Knysna National Lake Area

The 20km (12½-mile) or so Knysna lagoon is an eternally popular playground for golfers, boating enthusiasts, mountain-bikers, walkers and hikers. Oysters are cultivated here, served to the

Opposite, top to bottom:
The Augrabies landscape is dominated by dramatic cracked and weathered rock; colonies of Cape Gannets breed on Saldanha Bay's offshore islands; aloes, a fleshy succulent species at home in a rocky environment such as this on the Tsitsikamma coastline, are splendid in winter.

National Parks Guide

Proclaimed to protect indigenous coastal and limestone *fynbos* species (2000 plant species, over 110 of which appear on the IUCN Red List) and a rich local and migrant wetland bird life, including African Black Oystercatcher. Cape Agulhas is the southernmost tip of Africa, its treacherous coast dubbed the graveyard of ships after the multitude of wrecks littered here. Of interest are the Agulhas lighthouse museum and the shipwreck museum in nearby Bredasdorp.

public by the Knysna Oyster Company on Thesen Island, and there are trips on a paddle cruiser, the *John Benn* river boat or a catamaran, some stopping at the Featherbed Nature Reserve for its walking trails. Knysna's indigenous and cultivated forests at Harkerville and Diepwalle bristle with mountain-bikers and walkers. Water and forest bird life clocks up over 280 species.

Eastern Cape
Camdeboo National Park

The centrepiece of this relatively new national park is the 145km^2 (56-sq-mile) Karoo Nature Reserve encircling Graaff-Reinet, a charming town of over 200 19th-century national monument buildings. Partly straddling the Sneeuberg foothills, part low-lying plains ironed out to the Valley of Desolation, the latter is a truly dramatic section of the park, with resistant dolerite layers resulting in cracked and shattered pillars, pinnacles, buttresses and finely balanced boulders. The Vanryneveld's Pass dam has been renamed Nqweba; wildlife includes antelope and black wildebeest.

Tsitsikamma National Park

This 'place of much water' in the Khoisan tongue incorporates some 80km (50 miles) of spectacular rocky coastline and also extends 5km (3 miles) out to sea, protecting intertidal life, the reef and deep-sea fish. Common and bottlenose dolphins and southern right whales also pass by. Tsitsikamma is a space of verdant mountain slopes cleft by ravines thick with indigenous trees and restless waves hissing over a cracked rocky coastline. The park's boundaries have expanded over the years, the latest addition being Soetkraal, a dramatic skyline of unruly jagged peaks separated by the deep-valleyed Palmiet River. This 4x4 wilderness tract straddles the Tsitsikamma mountain range between Plettenberg Bay and Misgund in the Langkloof.

Northern Cape
Augrabies Falls National Park

This park focuses on the 56m (184ft) Augrabies Waterfall, sometimes full and thunderous, sometimes narrow and hemmed in by bare rock, on the Orange (Gariep) River which has forged an 18km (11-mile) gorge across the rocky landscape. On both the northern and southern sides of the Orange River, a 514km^2 (200-sq-mile)

Other South African National Parks

moonscape of quiver trees and fleshy succulents is the backdrop to springbok, gemsbok, giraffe and reintroduced black rhino.

Richtersveld National Park

This park has merged with Namibia's Ai-Ais Hot Springs Game Park, into which the Fish River Canyon falls, to create a massive 5086km² (1965-sq-mile) transfrontier territory. It is one of the largest conservation parks in Southern Africa. Border fences have been removed, and land is being leased from the local Nama, who continue to live and graze their livestock in the area. The Richtersveld is an austere, unrelenting landscape of sunburnt rock and desert sand, with the Gariep River yielding the only water. In spite of this, giant valleys gouged into ancient rock and presided over by shorn cliffs are extraordinary in their grandeur.

Limpopo
Marakele National Park

A merging of the original park, Welgevonden Game Reserve, and the privately owned Marakele contractual park, this 'place of sanctuary' in the Tswana language supports major species such as elephant, black and white rhino, roan and sable antelope and the big cats. Backed by the stony Waterberg and populated by twisted cedars, prehistoric-looking cycads and luxuriant tree ferns, the reserve is divided into the roughly 250km² (96-sq-mile) Kwaggasvlakte and the Greater Marakele National Park. Of special note are the cliffs' hundreds of breeding Cape Vultures, one of the world's largest colonies.

Namaqua National Park

A recent initiative by SANParks to protect the fragile ecosystems of Namaqualand, the greater Namaqua National Park embraces the Skilpad Wildflower Reserve, famous for its burnt-orange ursinia daisies. The park lies roughly 20km (12 miles) from Kamieskroon, with Springbok some 70km (45 miles) to the north. The topography that produces spring's sheets of wild flowers consists of granite terrain called Namaqualand Klipkoppe ('rocky heads'), part of a 50km (30-mile) fragmented mountain chain, and low-lying alluvial plains called the Sandveld. Namaqualand is home to the richest bulb flora of any arid region in the world and in spring, white, yellow and orange *gousblomme*, Namaqua daisies, beetle daisies, gazanias, and *vygies* unfurl across the landscape.

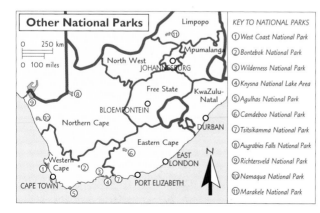

Other National Parks

Limpopo
⑪

0   250 km
0   100 miles

Mpumalanga

North West
JOHANNESBURG

Free State

KwaZulu-Natal

BLOEMFONTEIN

⑧

⑨

⑩

Northern Cape

DURBAN

Eastern Cape

EAST LONDON

Western Cape

⑥

N

PORT ELIZABETH

CAPE TOWN

① ② ③

④

⑤

KEY TO NATIONAL PARKS

① *West Coast National Park*
② *Bontebok National Park*
③ *Wilderness National Park*
④ *Knysna National Lake Area*
⑤ *Agulhas National Park*
⑥ *Camdeboo National Park*
⑦ *Tsitsikamma National Park*
⑧ *Augrabies Falls National Park*
⑨ *Richtersveld National Park*
⑩ *Namaqua National Park*
⑪ *Marakele National Park*

Travel Tips

How to get there

International airports exist in Johannesburg, Cape Town, Durban and outside Kruger Park. All have car-hire facilities and information centres.

Kruger National Park

The Kruger Mpumalanga International Airport (KMIA), situated 25km (16 miles) from the major centre of Nelspruit, is serviced daily from the Johannesburg and Cape Town airports by local carriers SA Express, SA Airlink and Nationwide. Private charters run by tour organizers operate from here too. International visitors can hire a car at KMIA to take them directly to Kruger National Park. Main gate entry points are Paul Kruger west of Skukuza, the reserve's headquarters, in the southern sector; Orpen, further north, in the central sector; and Malelane at the extreme south of the park. There are also two gates in the remote north, Punda Maria and Pafuri.

Visit: www.saexpress.co.za
www.saairlink.co.za
www.flynationwide.co.za

Car Hire

Major car hire companies include:
Avis, tel: 0861-113748 or +27-(0)11-9233660, www.avis.co.za
Budget, tel: 0861-016622 or +27-(0)11-3980123, www.budget.co.za
Europcar, tel: 0860-011344 or +27-(0)11-5744457, www.europcar.co.za

Road rules

In South Africa, driving is on the left-hand side of the road. The speed limit on national highways is 120kph (75mph), on secondary roads 100kph (60mph) and in urban areas 60kph (35mph). Camera and infra-red speed trapping is applied throughout the country.

Passports and visas

Visa requirements for anyone travelling to South Africa include the need for two consecutive blank pages (a left- and right-hand page) in your passport. The passport must also be valid for at least six months after the date of travel. If this is not the case, you will be prevented from boarding an aircraft or risk being deported when you arrive in South Africa. Note that a parent travelling with children but without the second parent needs to carry a police-certified letter of consent from the absent parent. Always carry photocopies of passport and visas, packed separately from the originals.

Health precautions

Malaria

A scourge of tropical and subtropical countries, malaria is caused by the female Anopheles mosquito, which pierces the skin to feed on high-protein blood necessary for her to reproduce. In this way she picks up the malaria parasite from an infected person, then spreads the disease every time she feeds on the blood of another person. Mosquitoes feed only at night, so protective measures are necessary only from dusk to dawn. Do note that most types of mosquito don't carry the malaria plasmodium (protoplasm), so being bitten doesn't necessarily mean that you will contract malaria.

Symptoms of malaria infection can manifest from anything between a week and three months after being bitten, and resemble flu-like conditions. Headaches and muscle ache, bouts of sweating, fever and chills are sometimes accompanied by diarrhoea, stomach ache and coughing. If left untreated, malaria can be fatal; it is crucial to inform the doctor that you've visited a malaria-risk area to avoid incorrect diagnosis.

The northern parts of the Limpopo and KwaZulu-Natal

Travel Tips

provinces carry the risk of malaria, therefore Kruger, Mapungubwe, the Greater St Lucia Wetland Area and Hluhluwe-iMfolozi parks are all affected. The crucial period is between December and April, the end of the rainy season. In South Africa, you can call the 24-hour malaria hotline on 082-2341800 for risks and advice on precautionary measures.

Taking prophylactics before and during travel is recommended. Consult a travel clinic before deciding on medication, as mosquitoes are known to become resistant to certain products. In South Africa, the most recommended prophylactic is a combination of Chloroquine (taken one week before travel) and Paludrin (taken daily two days before travel). Mefloquine (Lariam) used to be a single alternative but side effects of depression and hallucinations were reported, so beware of this product. In the USA, Chloroquine and Malarone are prescribed.

It is essential to fully complete the course of medication since the malarial incubation period can last up to a month after your safari trip. Pregnant women are advised not to visit malaria-infected areas.

Other preventive measures

- wear long sleeves, long trousers, socks and shoes in the early morning and evening to cover up the skin
- apply a mosquito repellent containing DEET (N,N-diethyl-meta-toluamide) to exposed skin every four hours
- use products containing citronella oil (creams, skin wipes, candles), although they are not considered as effective as DEET repellents. (Note: not recommended for young children or pregnant women.)
- burn mosquito coils, oils or electrically heated insecticide tablets in the bedroom at night
- sleep under a mosquito net (many lodges are equipped with nets)
- sleep under a moving fan, as mosquitoes struggle to fly where there is air movement.

Yellow fever

This doesn't apply to South Africa, but visitors entering from infected countries (for example, East Africa) may be required to produce an up-to-date yellow fever inoculation certificate. Check with your travel clinic.

Hepatitis A/B and tetanus

Hepatitis A is contractable from contaminated seafood, fruit, vegetables and water but is successfully prevented via vaccinations, one administered before travelling, the second six months later. Consult your travel clinic (check also for tetanus-diptheria). Hepatitis B is only transmitted via blood.

Bilharzia

Schistosomiasis, or bilharzia, is a waterborne parasite carried by snails. In Africa, particularly, it is a real threat in stagnant water areas of lakes, dams and slow-flowing rivers. Being on safari, though, means that many of the lakes and rivers are frequented by hippo and crocodile, preventing you anyway from swimming – but lodges and guides will always inform you of whether it's safe to swim.

Contacts

South Africa: Netcare Travel Clinics, www.travelclinic.co.za
USA: Centers for Disease Control and Prevention, www.cdc.gov
UK: www.travelhealth.co.uk

Drinking water

Throughout South Africa, particularly in the main cities and towns, tap water is chemically treated and perfectly safe to drink. In the rare cases where outlying areas are cautious about their

Travel Tips

water supply, bottled water is provided. Otherwise, bottled water is available wherever you travel, particularly on safari.

Electricity

South Africa uses 220/230 or 250 volts AC. Plugs are 5-amp two-pin or 15-amp round three-pin. Adapters may be required.

Sun and bug protection

The African sun is notoriously unforgiving, even in winter. Any trips into the bushveld, whether in an open 4x4 or on a walking trail, necessitate the wearing of a hat or peaked cap, good quality polaroid sunglasses and a high-SPF sunblock or sun protection cream. It may sound high, but skin experts insist that sun creams with an SPF of nothing less than 30 should be used. Apply sunscreen 30 minutes before going in the sun. The following items are also very useful on a safari trip:
• a moisturizing lip balm for chapped lips as bushveld air can be very drying
• an antibiotic ointment (e.g. Neosporin in South Africa) for cuts, insect bites or sores
• insect repellent containing the active ingredient DEET (N,N-diethyl-meta-toluamide) as liquid drops or a spray.

Although Africa is associated with snakes, scorpions, spiders, and insects, by taking a little care visitors are unlikely to be harmed by any of them. Snakes prefer to avoid human contact and will try to escape first; they retaliate only when directly threatened. If you venture outside your lodgings at night, wear sturdy closed shoes and take a torch. In certain safari areas, it's always a good idea to check shoes first for scorpions, as their tails can deliver a nasty sting. Most lodges and camps have insect-proof gauze or netting in the rooms.

When walking through long grass, wear long trousers to evade ticks, particularly a tiny, reddish hard-backed species that can transmit tick-bite fever; symptoms include constant headaches and fever. Always apply insect repellent to bare legs and arms.

Money matters

It is inadvisable to carry large amounts of cash when travelling. Most urban centres accept credit cards (Visa, Mastercard, AMEX, etc.) and traveller's cheques. Keep a list of traveller's cheque numbers separately with your belongings in the event of loss or theft. With the relaxation of exchange controls

it's now possible to make use of ATM cards at banks with international affiliations. One of the most recent innovations is a special prepaid travel debit card, used in the same way as an ATM card. You will need a certain amount of cash for smalls and shopping at local markets, but keep it safe in an internal zip pocket. Be extra wary of displaying any valuables, be they money, jewellery or photographic equipment.

Banking hours

Most banks are open 08:30 or 09:00–15:30 Monday to Friday, 08:30 or 09:00–11:00 on Saturday, closed Sunday.

VAT

Value Added Tax (VAT) stands at 14% and is levied on most commodities. Foreign visitors can claim back these monies on returning to their home countries by presenting the invoices, accompanied by the goods, at the airport.

Tipping

Part of the fabric of life in Africa … it is customary to tip porters, meter-taxi drivers, petrol attendants – and lately, the informal 'parking attendants'. Otherwise, a tip of between 10 and 15% of the bill for a meal in a cafetaria or restaurant is the going rate, depending of course on service. On safari, guides and trackers usually receive a tip (at private lodges, US$5–10 per person per day for guides; US$3–5 per person for trackers, given as a lump sum at the end of the stay).

Travel insurance

Despite technology and the sophistication of travel today, the risks of theft, accidents, illness, or forced changes to travel plans are as critical as ever. Taking out comprehensive travel insurance is a necessity. A good policy will, besides medical and accident-related issues, also cover legal assistance, help in contacting family, the replacing of travel documents, etc. Many credit card companies offer a degree of cover for holiday travel, but carefully check the extent of this cover. What's vital is good medical cover for evaluation of illness, hospitalization, treatment, and getting patients home.

Theft is a constant problem during travel. When flying, try to carry-on your valuables (including medication), although with the most recent terrorism scares, aircraft regulations are likely to vary depending on circumstances. Check regulations before

travelling. Always keep cameras and hand luggage within sight, whether at the airport or in a hotel foyer. Try to keep any belongings that are left in a vehicle out of sight; never ever leave bags, cameras or mobile phones lying visible on a seat.

Security while travelling

Travel Buddy: this mobile phone-based network with links to the SA Police, SA Tourist Association and relevant government departments was set up in 2003 by André Snyman. Visitors sign up by buying a SIM card at any phone shop at South African international airports, then register with Travel Buddy – or register via their website. Members are given a contact number to call day or night, and are constantly updated via SMS of any security threats and travel-related issues.
Tel: +27-(0)82-5611065
cellphone: 082-5611065
e-mail: webmaster@travelbuddy.co.za
web: www.travelbuddy.co.za

The national emergency phone number is 10111, which links to the police, medical/ambulance facilities and the fire department. The emergency numbers for cellphones are 112 (MTN and Virgin), 911 (Vodacom) and 148 (Cell-C).

Afrikaans Road Signs

Geen ingang
No entry
Lughawe
Airport
Ontvangs
Reception
Ingangshek
Entrance gate
Uitkykpunt
Lookout point
Uitklimpunt
Permission to leave vehicle
Parkeerterrein
Parking area
Piekniekplek
Picnic spot
Links
Left
Regs
Right
Ompad
Detour
Wildtuin
Game reserve
Natuurreservaat
Nature Reserve

Selected Animal and Bird Gallery

Elephant

White Rhino

Hippo

Buffalo

Blue Wildebeest

Banded Mongoose

Slender Mongoose

Dwarf Mongoose

Leopard Tortoise

Tree Squirrel

Burchell's Zebra

Rock Hyrax (Dassie)

Giraffe

Pangolin

Aardvark (Anteater)

Black-backed Jackal

Nile Crocodile

Warthog

Bushpig

Vervet Monkey

Aardwolf

Wild Dog

Chacma Baboon

Lesser Bushbaby

Samango Monkey

Animals

Lion

Cheetah

Caracal

Small-Spotted Genet

African Wild Cat

African Civet

Leopard

Serval

Springbok

Impala

Spotted Hyena

Brown Hyena

Reedbuck

Sharpe's Grysbok

Sable Antelope

Nyala

Kudu

Steenbok

Tsessebe

Gemsbok

Red Hartebeest

Bushbuck

Roan Antelope

Eland

Common Duiker

Klipspringer

Selected Animal and Bird Gallery

Fish Eagle

Crowned Eagle

Martial Eagle

Bateleur
Eagle

Tawny Eagle

Yellow-billed Kite

African Harrier
Hawk (Gymnogene)

Black-shouldered Kite

Paradise
Flycatcher

Gabar Goshawk

Black-
collared
Barbet

Crested Barbet

Black-eyed Bulbul

Fork-tailed
Drongo

Lanner
Falcon

Cape
Sugarbird

Kori Bustard

White-breasted
Cormorant

African
Hoopoe

Blue Waxbill

Birds

Greater Flamingo

Darter

White Pelican

African Black Oystercatcher

African (Jackass) Penguin

Cape Gannet

Egyptian Goose

Goliath Heron

Grey Heron

Brown-hooded Kingfisher

Pied Kingfisher

Hamerkop

Hadeda Ibis

Malachite Kingfisher

Giant Kingfisher

Threebanded Plover

Blue Crane

Marabou Stork

Saddle-billed Stork

African Jacana

Selected Animal and Bird Gallery

Trumpeter Hornbill

Ground Hornbill

Pied Babbler

Heuglin's Robin

Brown-headed Parrot

Glossy Starling

Purple-crested Lourie

Knysna Turaco

Secretary Bird

Orange-breasted Sunbird

Marico Sunbird

Spotted-backed Weaver

Narina Trogon

Scarlet-chested Sunbird

Redbilled Buffalo Weaver

Sociable Weaver

Longtailed Shrike

Purple Gallinule

Grey-headed Bush-shrike

Red-headed Weaver

Orange-breasted Bush-shrike

Birds

Giant Eagle Owl

Spotted Eagle Owl

Pel's Fishing Owl

Pearl-spotted Owlet

Ostrich

Jackal Buzzard

Pied Wagtail

Golden-tailed Woodpecker

Pintailed Whydah

Little Swift

Lammergeier

Helmeted Guineafowl

Cape Vulture

Lappet-faced Vulture

White-backed Vulture

Bokmakierie

Red-billed Oxpecker

Lilac-breasted Roller

Lesser Striped Swallow

Check list

Top Mammals
- Aardvark
- Aardwolf
- African wild cat
- African wild dog
- Bat-eared fox
- Black rhino
- Black wildebeest
- Black-backed jackal
- Black-footed (small-spotted) cat
- Blesbok
- Blue duiker
- Blue wildebeest
- Bontebok
- Brown hyena
- Buffalo
- Burchell's (Plains) zebra
- Bushbuck
- Bushpig
- Cape fur seal
- Cape mountain zebra
- Caracal
- Chacma baboon
- Cheetah
- Civet
- Common duiker
- Common reedbuck
- Eland
- Elephant
- Gemsbok
- Giraffe
- Greater bushbaby
- Grey duiker
- Grey rhebok
- Ground squirrel
- Grysbok
- Hippo
- Hyrax (Dassie)
- Impala
- Klipspringer
- Kudu
- Large-spotted genet
- Leopard
- Lesser bushbaby

- Lichtenstein's hartebeest
- Lion
- Lynx
- Mongoose
- Mountain reedbuck
- Nyala
- Oribi
- Pangolin
- Red duiker
- Red hartebeest
- Red squirrel
- Roan antelope
- Sable antelope
- Samango monkey
- Serval
- Spotted hyena
- Springbok
- Steenbok
- Striped polecat
- Suni
- Suricate (Meerkat)
- Thick-tailed bushbaby
- Tsessebe
- Vervet monkey
- Warthog
- Waterbuck
- White rhino

Top Reptiles
- Common barking gecko
- Crocodile
- Leatherback turtle
- Loggerhead turtle
- Monitor lizard
- Spiny agama
- Terrapin
- Tortoise

Top Birds
- African (Jackass) Penguin
- African Barred Owl
- African Black Oystercatcher
- African Fish Eagle
- African Goshawk
- African Hawk

- African Jacana
- African Rock Pipit
- African Scops Owl
- Alpine Swift
- Arrow-marked Babbler
- Bald Ibis
- Bank Cormorant
- Barratt's Warbler
- Bateleur Eagle
- Bearded Robin
- Bearded Woodpecker
- Bennett's Woodpecker
- Black Kite
- Black Swift
- Black Vulture
- Black-bellied Korhaan
- Black-breasted Snake Eagle
- Black-collared Barbet
- Black-headed Heron
- Black-shouldered Kite
- Blue Crane
- Böhm's Spinetail
- Bokmakierie
- Booted Eagle
- Brown Scrub Robin
- Brown Snake Eagle
- Brown-headed Parrot
- Brown-hooded Kingfisher
- Buff-spotted Flufftail
- Buff-streaked Chat
- Bulbul
- Cape Cormorant
- Cape Gannet
- Cape Parrot
- Cape Rock Thrush
- Cape Sugarbird
- Cape Vulture
- Carmine Bee-eater
- Chestnut-vented Tit-babbler
- Chorister Robin-chat
- Cinnamon Dove
- Cinnamon-breasted Bunting
- Crested Barbet
- Crimson-breasted Shrike
- Crowned Cormorant
- Crowned Eagle

Check list

- [ ] Crowned Hornbill
- [ ] Denham's (Stanley's) Bustard
- [ ] Eastern Clapper
- [ ] Eastern Nicator
- [ ] Fairy Flycatcher
- [ ] Fiscal Flycatcher
- [ ] Forest Canary
- [ ] Fork-tailed Drongo
- [ ] Gabar Goshawk
- [ ] Giant Kingfisher
- [ ] Golden-rumped Tinker Barbet
- [ ] Goliath Heron
- [ ] Grass Owl
- [ ] Greater Flamingo
- [ ] Green Coucal
- [ ] Grey Cuckoo-shrike
- [ ] Grey-headed Seagull
- [ ] Grey-hooded Kingfisher
- [ ] Ground Hornbill
- [ ] Ground Woodpecker
- [ ] Gymnogene
- [ ] Hartlaub's Seagull
- [ ] Helmeted Guineafowl
- [ ] Heuglin's Robin
- [ ] Jackal Buzzard
- [ ] Karoo Eremomola
- [ ] Karoo Korhaan
- [ ] Karoo Scrub Robin
- [ ] Kelp Seagull
- [ ] Knysna Turaco
- [ ] Kori Bustard
- [ ] Lammergeier (Bearded Vulture)
- [ ] Lanner Falcon
- [ ] Lappet-faced Vulture
- [ ] Lazy Cisticola
- [ ] Lemon-breasted Canary
- [ ] Lesser Flamingo
- [ ] Lesser Masked Weaver
- [ ] Lesser Spotted Eagle
- [ ] Lilac-breasted Roller

- [ ] Little Sparrowhawk
- [ ] Ludwig's Bustard
- [ ] Malachite Kingfisher
- [ ] Malachite Sunbird
- [ ] Marabou Stork
- [ ] Martial Eagle
- [ ] Melodious Lark
- [ ] Meyer's Parrot
- [ ] Mocking Chat
- [ ] Montagu's Harrier
- [ ] Namaqua Warbler
- [ ] Narina Trogon
- [ ] Open-billed Stork
- [ ] Orange-breasted Bush Shrike
- [ ] Orange-breasted Rockjumper
- [ ] Orange-breasted Sunbird
- [ ] Osprey
- [ ] Ostrich
- [ ] Pale Chanting Goshawk
- [ ] Pallid Harrier
- [ ] Palm-nut Vulture
- [ ] Pearl-spotted Owl
- [ ] Pel's Fishing Owl
- [ ] Pied Babbler
- [ ] Pied Kingfisher
- [ ] Pink Twin-spot
- [ ] Pink-backed Pelican
- [ ] Pririt Batis
- [ ] Purple Gallinule
- [ ] Purple-crested Turaco
- [ ] Pygmy Falcon
- [ ] Pygmy Goose
- [ ] Racket-tailed Roller
- [ ] Red-billed Francolin
- [ ] Red-billed Wood Hoopoe
- [ ] Red-crested Korhaan
- [ ] Red-fronted Tinker Barbet
- [ ] Rock Kestrel
- [ ] Roseate Tern
- [ ] Rosy-faced Lovebird
- [ ] Rudd's Apalis
- [ ] Rufous-bellied Heron
- [ ] Rufous-cheeked Nightjar

- [ ] Saddle-billed Stork
- [ ] Scarlet-chested Sunbird
- [ ] Secretary Bird
- [ ] Shaft-tailed Whydah
- [ ] Sickle-winged Chat
- [ ] Sociable Weaver
- [ ] Southern Ground Hornbill
- [ ] Southern Masked Weaver
- [ ] Southern Tchagra
- [ ] Southern White-faced Scops Owl
- [ ] Spoonbill
- [ ] Spotted Eagle Owl
- [ ] Steppe Buzzard
- [ ] Steppe Eagle
- [ ] Stierling's Barred Warbler
- [ ] Striped Kingfisher
- [ ] Swee Waxbill
- [ ] Tambourine Dove
- [ ] Tawny Eagle
- [ ] Thick-billed Cuckoo
- [ ] Thick-billed Lark
- [ ] Three-streaked Tchagra
- [ ] Tropical Boubou
- [ ] Trumpeter Hornbill
- [ ] Twin Greenspot
- [ ] Verreaux's (Black) Eagle
- [ ] Verreaux's (Giant) Eagle Owl
- [ ] Violet-eared Waxbill
- [ ] Wahlberg's Eagle
- [ ] Wailing Cisticola
- [ ] Wattle-eyed Flycatcher
- [ ] White Pelican
- [ ] White-backed Vulture
- [ ] White-breasted Cormorant
- [ ] White-browed Robin-chat (Heuglin's Robin)
- [ ] White-eared Barbet
- [ ] White-faced Owl
- [ ] White-faced Scops Owl
- [ ] White-winged Korhaan
- [ ] Woodward's Batis
- [ ] Yellow-bellied Eremomola
- [ ] Yellow-billed Kite
- [ ] Yellow-billed Stork
- [ ] Yellow-spotted Nicator

Index

Index

Imprint Page

First edition published in 2007
by New Holland Publishers (UK) Ltd
London • Cape Town • Sydney • Auckland
10 9 8 7 6 5 4 3 2 1

website: www.newhollandpublishers.com

Garfield House, 86 Edgware Road
London W2 2EA
United Kingdom

80 McKenzie Street
Cape Town 8001
South Africa

Unit 1, 66 Gibbes Street
Chatswood, NSW 2067
Australia

218 Lake Road
Northcote, Auckland
New Zealand

Distributed in the USA by
The Globe Pequot Press, Connecticut

ISBN 978 1 84537 559 1

Although every effort has been made to ensure that
this guide is up to date and current at time of going to
print, the Publisher accepts no responsibility or liability
for any loss, injury or inconvenience incurred by
readers or travellers using this guide.

Keep us Current
Information in travel guides is apt to change, which is
why we regularly update our guides. We'd be grateful
to receive feedback if you've noted something we
should include in our updates. If you have new
information, please share it with us by writing to the
Publishing Manager, Globetrotter, at the office nearest
to you (addresses on this page). The most significant
contribution to each new edition will receive a free
copy of the updated guide.

Publishing Manager: Thea Grobbelaar
DTP Cartographic Manager: Genené Hart
Editor: Thea Grobbelaar
Design and DTP: Nicole Bannister
Cartographer: Nicole Bannister
Picture Researcher: Shavonne Govender
Illustrators: Steven Felmore (birds), Michael Thayer
(reptiles), Penny Meakin & Michael Thayer (mammals)

Reproduction by Resolution, Cape Town
Printed and bound by Star Standard Industries (Pte)
Ltd, Singapore

Photographic credits:
Africa Imagery: half title page, title page, pages 52
(top), 52 (centre), 55, 98 (top), 120, 126, 131; **Shaen
Adey/IOA:** contents page, pages 6 (bottom), 72 (centre), 88 (centre), 95, 96, 98 (bottom), 112 (top), 119,
134 (bottom), 142 (centre); **Tony Camaco/IOA:**
page 6 (centre); **Colour Library/IOA:** pages 62 (bottom), 69, 78; **Roger de la Harpe/IOA:** page 86;
Nigel Dennis/IOA: front cover, back cover (top, centre and bottom), pages 13, 23, 32 (bottom), 34, 52
(bottom), 61, 62 (top), 67, 70, 72 (bottom), 88 (bottom), 142 (top); **Gerhard Dreyer/IOA:** pages 20
(right), 112 (centre); **Martin Harvey/IOA:** page 48;
Leonard Hoffman/IOA: page 134 (centre); **Walter
Knirr/IOA:** pages 24 (centre), 29, 31, 72 (top), 80, 85,
103, 114, 117, 134 (top); **Peter Pickford/IOA:** page
59; **Carol Polich/IOA:** pages 24 (top and bottom),
26; **Jonathan Reid/IOA:** pages 125 (top), 130;
Erhardt Thiel/IOA: pages 112 (bottom), 123;
Ariadne van Zandbergen/IOA: pages 32 (top), 50,
107, 111, 125 (bottom); **Friedrich von
Hörsten/IOA:** page 62 (centre); **Hein von
Hörsten/IOA:** pages 9, 14, 20 (left), 125 (centre),
129, 136, 142 (bottom); **Lanz von Hörsten/
IOA:** pages 6 (top), 18, 32 (centre), 38, 41, 47;
Andrew Woodburn/IOA: page 98 (centre); **Keith
Young/IOA:** pages 43, 88 (top).
[**IOA** = Images of Africa]

Cover: *Leopard (front); giraffe, Bateleur Eagle, hippo
(back, top to bottom).*
Half title page: *A majestic red hartebeest.*
Title page: *Giraffe towering over the vegetation.*